Katharina von der Leyen

Puppies

Selection and Character ● Training and Games
Feeding and Care ● Health

BARRON'S

Every dog should have a master of its own. There is nothing like having a well-behaved human around who fluffs up your bed or puts down your supper when you get home dog tired after work.
Corey Ford

So, You Want a Dog

Nothing is easier than falling in love with a puppy. It's not always easy to keep a level head when the object of your desire is warm, fuzzy, and cuddly and fits into your lap just right. One look from those large, moist eyes, and your willpower melts like butter. It's not your fault; you can't help it. Probably our ancestors tens of thousands of years ago had the same reaction when *Canis familiaris*, wet-nosed and tail-wagging, weaseled its way into the heart of *Homo sapiens*.

It's not quite so easy to love the puppy a little later when—at least for the first six months—you have to get up every morning before six (six-thirty, if you are lucky) to march outside in your pajamas, clutching the little beast that has to urinate. Having relieved itself, it thinks 6:30 A.M. is the perfect time to start the day with some wild dashing around and playing.

It's easy to love a puppy when, exhausted and cute, it falls asleep in your lap. It's not so easy when you have just spent the last three hours picking up feathers from a big pillow the puppy attacked with great ferocity and unfortunately tore to ribbons while you took a well-deserved nap. It's easy to love your puppy when people keep stopping you on the street every two minutes to tell you how cute and adorable the little creature on the other end of the leash is—but remember how you felt when your little sweetheart had an attack of diarrhea on the bedroom rug. Having a dog means having one more family member with the need to be loved, fed, and kept healthy. You'll be aware of this very acutely at those moments when you feel you have not a minute to spare, not even to pet your puppy's ears.

Don't think you know all about it because you had a dog at home when you were a child. As a child, you had only the faintest idea of the effort and trouble involved in having a pet; in a pinch it was your parents who took care of the dog. Besides, nothing is the way it used to be. Nowadays dogs are too demanding, and you can't simply let them out anymore to take care of their needs. (Today, Thomas Mann's dog Baschan in the story "A Man and His Dog" would be shot by the warden without qualms if it was caught chasing rabbits, and its well-intentioned literary master would be notified of the fact by mail.) A dog waiting at the bus stop for its human playmate to come home from school would be taken to the animal shelter if it did not get run over before ever reaching the bus stop. Life is no longer the way it used to be. Dogs live with families that juggle busy schedules of work, school, judo lessons, and math tutoring, all of which leaves little time for dog walks. There is less time in the modern world, and there is also less space, less space for people and dogs, and for chickadees and rabbits. A modern dog has to learn to live in an apartment and to control its natural urges; it has to learn to walk on the leash without pulling, to lie down where it is told to, to bark at the door but only if there is good reason for it, not to jump up on furniture, and to come when called. A modern dog has to learn not to urinate on the floor but to wait until it is let out, not to run away, not to defend its food, and not to bite children who stick M&Ms up its nose. For a modern dog to be able to live up to our expectations we have to learn to understand it and to treat it well and with fairness. And don't think this is so obvious that it doesn't need mentioning.

So before you take that soft little bundle of a puppy home with you and make it part of your life you have to ask yourself—and answer—a number of questions. Consider carefully what having a dog means for you, your family, and your way of life. Keeping a dog is not a simple matter; it takes more than you might think.

German Wirehaired Pointer

Contents

Your Puppy's Health 103

Training 127

Appendix 153

Tables and Sidebars on the Most Important Topics

Introduction

What You Need to Have a Dog

What do you need to have a dog? To start with you need money. **Dogs are expensive.** First of all there is the money you have to pay for the dog. If you get a puppy from friends whose dog has had a litter you probably won't have to pay anything at all. Getting a dog from an animal shelter will cost you about $100 to $200, and if you buy from a breeder you may have to pay anywhere from $300 to $2,000, depending on the dog's breed.

Unfortunately your expenses do not come to an end when you pack up your puppy and take it home. Almost immediately you will have to pay a veterinarian's bill for the last set of immunizations if your puppy hasn't had them yet or for a general check-up. Even if you have a full-grown, healthy dog you have to figure on a sizable sum every year for vaccinations, check-ups, and medications against parasites like fleas, ticks, and worms. Also, ear infections and skin problems have a way of turning up at the most inconvenient times.

Add to this the cost of liability insurance, which you should definitely get for your dog. Just imagine your dog running across the road, a truck veering to the side trying to avoid hitting the dog and crashing through a store front. True, this is an unlikely scenario, but it could conceivably happen. A more realistic danger is that your dog may someday, in a fit of more or less justified fury, puncture the ear of your neighbor's fat canine. The incident would be much less upsetting if you could call your neighbor and assure her that your insurance will pay for any necessary veterinary services.

Then there is the fee for the dog license, which varies in different localities and is multiplied by the number of dogs living in your household. In many cases there will later be a bill for neutering, a bill whose amount depends on the dog's size and the veterinarian's fee schedule.

And from the day you bring your puppy home there will be the cost of dog food, the costs of which vary according to the size of your dog and the quality of food being purchased. You will undoubtedly be unable to resist buying boxes of dog biscuits and delicacies like dried pig's ears and rawhide treats, so you should for accuracy's sake include a few extra dollars a month in the food budget.

And it goes on, with the purchase of various items like a dog bed, collar, leash, and brush, food dishes, toys, and dog books, all of which will add up to another sizable sum. If you have a dog that has to be trimmed, you should add the cost of at least two visits to the canine

beauty parlor a year—or, if you plan to do the job yourself, the cost of electric clippers. If you travel quite a bit and have no cooperative friend or nice aunt who will look after your dog while you are away, you will also have to budget stays at the kennel, which vary in cost. And in more cases than you might think as a new dog owner there will be another important expense that is more than justified, namely, obedience training. This can be quite costly. Sometimes resorting to professional dog training is the only way a dog owner is able to regain control over his or her own life.

Be sure to read your homeowner's restrictions, covenants, or terms of your lease. Most standard leases contain a clause that forbids the keeping of pets, but it is always possible to discuss the matter with your landlord. If the answer is no, you will either have to find another apartment or give up your dream of having a dog. The law in such cases always sides with the landlord.

And then, of course, you need time and patience. Time and patience to get

Irish Setters

your puppy housebroken, to feed it at least three times a day, to brush it, go for walks with it, play with it, take it to the veterinarian, to train it, pet it, talk to it, and love it.

Don't say that you know all about the time it takes. Going outside with the puppy every two hours and waiting in the pouring rain or the sub-zero cold until it is ready is anything but pleasant, and your patience will be tried to the breaking point when you get up some morning and step into a puddle with your bare feet because the dog forgot that it has been housebroken for weeks. It's not easy to spend hours teaching the animal to *sit!* and *come!* and to remain patient and positive the whole time. It can be infuriating to issue those commands in the presence of friends and have the dog look at you as if you had taken leave of your senses.

You may feel like strangling it when, after you have spent hours cleaning the house, it races in looking as though it had just taken a mud bath, runs through the entire apartment, then throws up on the living room

rug and leaves paw prints all over the sofa. It's not easy, especially at moments like these, to overcome your annoyance and bandage a bleeding paw or take the dog's temperature rectally or find a veterinarian in the middle of the night.

Time and patience. If you are short on time and even shorter on patience, that is very understandable and no problem at all, but perhaps you should take it as a hint that you might be better off with a different kind of pet—a bird, a rabbit, or perhaps fish.

If you do have all the time and patience in the world, there is still one other important factor to be considered, and that is *love*. You may fully intend to love your dog in sickness and in health; but just as when we pronounce these words before the altar in the best of faith and with utter conviction, we really don't quite realize what it is we are promising. Like a marriage partner, a dog is a totally different being; it is in fact a being of a different species. In this case, you are the more intelligent of the two,

and consequently you have to love your dog and communicate with it in such a way that it may understand what you mean. You have to learn its language because it can't speak yours.

Every time you interact with your dog, talk to it, ask it to do something, you have to try to imagine what its eyes can see and its brain can comprehend. A dog's interpretation of the world is almost always fundamentally different from yours, and it's the dog's interpretation that matters. You have to learn to communicate with your dog in a way it can understand and learn to recognize what it thinks. This sounds more difficult than it actually is, and, as in most marriages, it takes only a few misunderstandings for us to learn to read the other's thoughts and understand a point-of-view that is foreign to ours. (This shows that keeping a dog can, among many other things, teach us some important lessons for life.)

You have to recognize your dog for what it is. It is not a small, fur-covered person. Its view of the world is entirely different from

Introduction

yours, and it thinks differently from you. It is a much less complex being, with very basic instincts and very basic reactions. Its physical and mental abilities and potential are limited, and you have to learn to recognize these limits, so you will ask neither too much nor too little of it.

Reasons for Not Getting a Dog

There are plenty of reasons not to get a dog, and I personally keep thinking of new ones almost every day, when, for instance, hail is pelting down and I have to take my dog out in spite of it, or when I have to dig my terrier out of a rabbit hole in below-freezing temperatures, or when my dog insists on going out just when I have hit my stride working on the computer, or when I'm late leaving the house and my Pug tears my stockings in a fit of affection.

It is *not* a good idea to get a dog for a child in hopes of teaching the child a sense of responsibility. Children are unable to keep the promises they make—just remember the various dolls

your daughter could not live without and that now lie buried in the sandbox minus hair and eyelashes and perhaps even without a head, or the electric train that had to be purchased and is now packed away in heavy boxes in the cellar, covered with a thick layer of dust. Buy a dog only if it is primarily you who wants one. If you want to live with a dog, then by all means get one.

Taking the dog for walks is *your* responsibility; so is feeding it, grooming it, and petting it. If there is someone who wants to help with all this, all the better. But you should want a dog at least as much as everyone else in the family, because you will probably be stuck with most of its care. If you take on the responsibility with mixed feelings, you will only be teaching your children that looking after a dog is a nuisance.

Another reason for not getting a dog is that though you would like to have one you have to work such long hours or you have so many other hobbies that there simply is not enough time left for the dog.

Or you love white furniture and don't like dog hair on the carpets and your clothes.

Or you want a dog to guard the house but not really be part of the family.

Or you have to travel a lot professionally and are unable to take the dog along on your trips.

If you are someone who needs a lot of time alone or who sometimes simply can't stand having another creature around constantly, don't get a dog. A dog always wants to be where you are, demands attention, and would like to be told what everything is all about.

If this kind of behavior gets on your nerves, maybe you should consider getting a cat, an animal whose personality is more like yours. Respect for other creatures includes recognizing and satisfying their needs, different as they may be from yours.

You have every right to decide against having a dog, and sometimes it's a good idea to simply postpone the decision for a while. The more seriously potential dog owners think about what kind of dog would suit them

Basset Hound

best and at what point in their lives they should get one, the better for the dogs of the world. There might not be any need anymore for animal shelters.

Maybe you have some idea now of what you are about to embark on.

And what does a dog owner get in return?

The Right Dog

Dog owners have a rosy complexion because they are out in the open air so much. They have the good fortune of living with an idealist, for dogs think life is wonderful, and some of that rubs off. If you have a dog, you won't need a guru, for dogs always live in the present. They are

spontaneity personified, and that is probably why we love dogs so much. They love the same things we do but have more time to enjoy them. Dogs don't like to be alone; they love laughter, games, dumb jokes, and social gatherings of all kinds. My dogs often start racing around like crazy when there is a party in the house,

13

Siberian Huskies

Introduction

performing tricks without being asked to, and clearly having a good time for no particular reason we can see. They simply feel the good cheer around them, and it makes them so happy that they can't help frolicking.

Dogs and humans seem made for each other: Dogs love to be scratched, and the human hand is a perfect scratching device. When you're watching television, dogs love to lie in your lap, snoring so loudly that you can barely hear the news, but to make up for what you miss they accompany you enthusiastically to the mailbox or the cellar. A dog is probably the most selfless friend you will ever have. As long as it is allowed to be near you all is well. Dogs are also a wonderful means to self-knowledge; not only are they usually the mirror image of their owner, but they also demonstrate constantly what human beings should be like—and what they should not be like.

Dogs and humans have been intimately linked in mutual affection for over 20,000 years, and everybody is aware how much we have changed dogs genetically to match our wishes and ideas. I am firmly convinced, however, that dogs have changed us too. Because dogs have always had more acute senses of hearing and smelling, we could concentrate on seeing. And because most dogs are courageous and brave, we could afford to let our adrenal glands shrink. And finally, with the aid of dogs we became more effective hunters, and so we have had more time to think. In short, dogs have made us into better humans.

Dogs come in more shapes, colors, and sizes than you can imagine. No other species offers you more possibilities to find a custom fit. There are over 400 dog breeds and consequently innumerable different canine personalities, and that doesn't even take into account mongrels, which can combine the genes of the most diverse breeds. This variety of offerings is wonderful but also over-whelming. How is anyone to find his or her ideal dog?

To find a perfect dog you have to examine yourself first of all. Make a list of the things that matter to you above all else, then of things that are not so crucial, and finally of things you can't stand. If the most important thing in your life is the flower garden you tend with loving care, you would probably be better off with a dignified Pekingese or a lively miniature Spitz than with a terrier because terriers are practically programmed for digging work. If the Old English Sheepdog appeals to you because of its long, shaggy coat and its goofy personality, be aware that keeping its luxuriant silky coat looking good takes several hours of brushing a week or the financial means to take the dog regularly to a doggy beauty parlor. And the owner has to have an unshakable sense of humor along with the ability to keep control over this canine clown in spite of the demands of family and job. Might not a Labrador Retriever that can simply be washed be a better choice?

Find out what a particular breed was originally developed for. In a time when so many people explore their family roots, it is amazing

Italian Greyhound

how few are interested in researching the roots of their dogs. An astonishing number of otherwise highly educated people have no idea for what purpose their dog was bred many centuries ago. Yet they might have much less trouble with their dogs and be able to avoid or solve many behavioral problems if they knew the background of the breed.

Even though you may think that most Irish Setters have not been used for hunting in ages, there has been no concomitant change in the genetic predisposition of your dog.

A Borzoi, which is a greyhound, may no longer get a chance to hunt wolves—especially in countries where those predators have long since been exterminated—but that does not affect its urge to sprint for miles across open fields.

Most modern-day indoor Jack Russells no longer have any need to dive into narrow burrows after foxes or martens, but that does not mean that they have lost their taste for exploring rabbit hutches.

You can't blame your Westie for killing your pet hamster—it is a terrier, and eliminating rodents is a terrier's job. (My terrier, Bella, keeps trying to break into the aquarium of a friend of mine because she wants to get rid of an utterly harmless catfish. To Bella, the fish is a mouse and consequently an enemy.)

Don't be surprised if your Newfoundland goes swimming in your neighbor's swimming pool whenever it gets a chance; its original job was swimming to save people.

Siberian Huskies and other sled dogs were bred to pull ahead with all their strength, dragging heavy sleds through deep snow. Is it surprising then that many urban Husky owners have a hard time teaching their dogs to heel?

Find out all you can about the breeds you are interested in; this way you will be able to avoid many problems before they arise. Or at least you won't be surprised.

If you travel a lot and would like to take your canine companion along,

you should consider a smaller dog. You'll have an easier time getting a hotel room with three Pugs than with one Rottweiler. A large dog requires a bigger car and stronger nerves because other people tend to be scared of big dogs. Feeding a big dog also costs more. Small dogs are often yappers but on the whole are easier to take care of. You can usually take a small dog along to a friend's house, whereas a Newfoundland takes up as much room as a piano. Besides, smaller dogs (they don't have to be the tiniest toy size) are generally easier for first-time owners.

Smaller dogs are easier to train; many things that are essential to teach a big dog are of no practical consequence for small dogs. A Dachshund will find it much more difficult to steal food from the kitchen counter than a Setter. (If a Dachshund or a Yorkshire Terrier manages this trick, the dog is a genius and almost deserves praise for its ingenuity.) If you can't teach your dog not to jump up on people, the consequences are not as

Wolf Spitz

serious in the case of a small dog as of a large one. Even an aggressive dog is easier to handle if it is small than if it is large.

Don't pay as much attention to the appearance of the dog you are interested in as to its character. Most people care more about whether the dog they are getting will tolerate children or go jogging with their significant other than whether or not its ancestors really go back to some aboriginal tribe of Tasmania. Whether the dog will play peacefully with other dogs in the park is of more practical importance than the fact that its grandam was world champion seven times in a row. Whether or not a dog sheds like a mohair sweater is more important than the exact length of its spine. The color of the eyes is inconsequential when compared to possible visual defects. And if it so happens that the beautiful dog you have dreamed of all your life turns out to be the least compatible in terms of personality, that is just too bad.

The most gorgeous

Cavalier King Charles Spaniels

dog will get on your nerves terribly if its character doesn't jibe with yours. Vice versa, the dumpiest looking pooch will appear to you in the most glowing light if your life together works out like hand in glove. (I have yet to meet a male model who could keep me awake for more than half an hour with his fascinating discourse, and I can't think of any artist or composer whose physical beauty was comparable to his talent.)

Think about whether the dog that appeals to you fits your life circumstances. A dog that is right for a family with three adolescent boys who spend all their free time playing football and wrestling will be the wrong choice for a quiet couple that is happiest playing bridge. If you are interested in a purebred dog, choosing will be relatively easy because these dogs have been developed for centuries to embody specific character qualities. The problem is

Introduction

more difficult with mixed breeds because you can never know exactly which genes predominate in a little puppy—the mother's or the father's—and there may be no telling who the grandparents were. The advantage of getting a purebred dog is that, as a result of selective breeding, it is born with a fixed genetic makeup, and we know what it will look like

when full-grown and what its genetically determined character qualities are.

There are also advantages to getting a mongrel dog rather than a purebred. Dogs whose parentage has been mixed for at least eight or ten generations are less susceptible to hereditary diseases, whereas the hybrid offspring of two purebred dogs may inherit the worst

of both parents' genes. The reverse is also true; they may inherit the best of each parent. First generation crossbreeds' genetics aren't well understood, but sometimes progeny work out well. An example: Crossing Labs with Golden Retrievers in certain guide dog breeding programs. Mongrels often have a less clearly defined character than purebred

Fox Terriers

dogs, which tend to have very strongly developed temperaments; they are *very* friendly, *very* independent, *very* eager to hunt, *very* energetic, and so on.

I think mixed breeds are wonderful dogs, and I have had many in the course of my life. My dog Bella is part Jack Russell and part Lhasa Apso; however, her Lhasa heritage (calmness, restraint, Tibetan wisdom) seems to have gotten lost somewhere along the line, and she is pure terrier except for her fur, which is too long. If I thought I was getting a dog with a diminished hunting instinct (Lhasa Apsos have about as much interest in hunting as a foot stool) I was clearly mistaken. I can't count the nights I have spent tromping through the woods with a flashlight looking for my little dog, nor do I care to estimate the volume of earth I have shoveled into holes she has dug in the garden in pursuit of voles and mice.

Any puppy that is not purebred has genes deriving from so many sources that picking the dog that will be right for you and your family is far from easy. In fact, for someone having little experience with dogs it may be a matter of pure luck. But no matter what the situation, there are strategies for finding a puppy that will suit you.

Now let's look at some basic information on dog breeds and their character-istics.

Rhodesian Ridgebacks

Dog Breeds and Their Characteristics

Breed Class	**Pointers**	**Burrowing Dogs**

Examples	◆ German Wirehaired Pointer Weimaraner ◆ Vizsla ◆ Grosser Münsterländer ◆ Irish Setter	◆ Dachshund ◆ Jack Russell Terrier ◆ Fox Terrier
Breed characteristics	◆ outstanding nose ◆ excellent hearing ◆ strong hunting instinct ◆ ferocious toward prey ◆ ready subordination	◆ ferocious toward prey ◆ strong hunting instinct ◆ high pain threshold ◆ independence
Desirable traits deriving from breed character	◆ ability to adapt ◆ little aggressiveness toward humans ◆ eagerness to learn ◆ intelligence	◆ great personality ◆ sense of humor
Undesirable traits deriving from breed character	◆ chase game on their own ◆ great need to be kept busy ◆ require a great deal of exercise	◆ yappers ◆ hard to train ◆ like to dig everywhere

Fighting Dogs

- Staffordshire Terrier
- Pit Bull Terrier
- Bull Terrier

- high pain threshold
- great physical strength
- ability to adapt

- little aggressiveness
  toward humans

- tendency to fight
  other dogs
- don't like to subordinate
  themselves to other dogs

Companion Dogs

- Chihuahua
- Havanese
- Dalmatian
- Chow Chow
- French Bulldog
- Pug
- Poodle
- Maltese
- Pekingese

- devotion to humans
- small size
- ability to adapt

- restrained temperament
- friendly toward children
- easy to get along with

- sometimes yappers
- get bored easily if not
  kept busy enough

Breed Class	**Herding Dogs**	**Greyhounds**

Examples	◆ Briard ◆ Collie ◆ Puli ◆ Corgi ◆ Old English Sheepdog ◆ Sheltie ◆ German Shepherd	◆ Afghan Hound ◆ Whippet ◆ Greyhound ◆ Borzoi ◆ Saluki ◆ Irish Wolfhound
Breed characteristics	◆ independence ◆ intelligence ◆ aggressive in defense ◆ love of exercise ◆ eager to work	◆ excellent sight ◆ hunting instinct ◆ independence ◆ speed ◆ sense of humor
Desirable traits resulting from breed character	◆ intelligence ◆ eagerness to learn	◆ very little barking ◆ hardly any aggressiveness toward humans
Undesirable traits resulting from breed character	◆ great need to be kept busy ◆ often destructive when not challenged enough	◆ disobedience ◆ urge to hunt ◆ oversensitive ◆ nervousness ◆ need a great deal of exercise

Guard Dogs

- Spitz
- Doberman
- Boxer
- Saint Bernard
- Bernese Mountain Dog
- Rottweiler
- Schnauzer
- Great Dane

- great alertness
- excellent hearing
- aggressive in defense
- stay close to home

- no urge to hunt
- suspicious of strangers
- intelligence

- aggressiveness toward strangers
- yappers
- training has to be very varied because of the dogs' high intelligence
- sometimes possessive

Hounds

- Beagle
- Foxhound
- Basset Hound

- independence
- outstanding nose
- strong hunting instinct

- very little aggressiveness
- friendly toward children
- very easy to get along with

- little bonding with one individual (love everybody)
- difficult to train
- will follow scents and game on their own for miles

Breed Class

Retrievers

Examples

◆ Golden Retriever
◆ Labrador Retriever
◆ Cocker Spaniel

Breed characteristics

◆ independence
◆ love of water
◆ hunting instinct

Desirable traits resulting from breed character

◆ practically no aggression toward humans
◆ obedient
◆ eager to learn
◆ excellent working dogs (for customs, as seeing eye dogs)

Undesirable traits resulting from breed character

◆ great need to be kept busy
◆ very accepting and therefore friendly toward everybody

Nordic Dogs

Terriers

Nordic Dogs	Terriers
◆ Siberian Husky	◆ Airedale
◆ Samoyed	◆ Irish
◆ Shiba Inu	◆ Border
◆ Alaskan Malamute	◆ Skye
◆ Eurasian	◆ Cairn
	◆ West Highland White

◆ intelligence	◆ strong character
◆ independence	◆ strong hunting instinct
◆ hunting instinct	◆ intelligence
	◆ ferocious toward prey

◆ suspicious of strangers	◆ playful
◆ very playful	◆ cheerful
◆ hardly ever bark	◆ very active
	◆ learn fast

◆ great need to be kept busy	◆ obstinate
◆ tend to be obstinate	◆ often hard to train
◆ can be hard to train	◆ some dogs have strong urge to hunt
	◆ some dogs hunt on their own
	◆ aggressive
	◆ often short-tempered with children

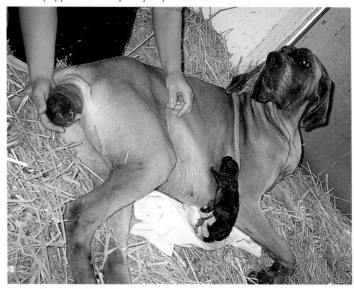

The Developmental Stages of Puppies

One look at the fuzzy face of a puppy, at its bright eyes, and at its permanently wagging little tail is enough to bewitch you, melt your heart, and deprive you of the ability to formulate a clear thought. Grownups have been known to lie flat on the floor, murmur endless baby talk, let fat little puppies crawl all over them, and put up with having their ears washed by pink, wet puppy tongues. Try, all the same, to take a deep breath and have a close look at the puppies. Remember that in six months these irresistible little balls of fuzz will look and act like completely different animals.

It is important to understand the different phases of development of a puppy so that you will be prepared for the changes your dog will undergo as it grows up. Everything that happens or fails to happen during these phases has a profound influence on the behavior of the adult dog.

Birth

Born with eyes and ears closed, puppies are completely dependent on their mother. At birth, their body temperature is about 103° Fahrenheit (39.5° C). They can't maintain this temperature on their own and therefore always seek the physical closeness of their mother or their warm siblings. Their bodies are about 84 percent water. Their heart rate is often over 200 beats per minute. Most of the nervous system is still rudimentary. They live in a world they can neither see nor hear yet, and they sleep

At birth puppies are completely dependent on their mother.

about 90 percent of the time. Their behavior is determined by reflexes they are born with, such as suckling, crawling, being drawn to warmth, and uttering sounds of distress when feeling hunger, cold, or pain. Urinating and defecating are reflex actions stimulated only when the mother massages their belly and anus by licking.

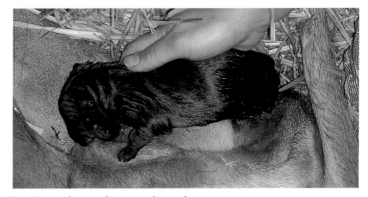

Puppies are born with eyes and ears shut.

Day 5

The nervous system develops very quickly. Puppies that are picked up at this age straighten their backs and stretch out their legs instead of curling up into the shape of a comma. Their eyes are still tightly closed, and they don't look much like dogs yet. They might be taken for sleeping guinea pigs.

Day 5: At this point they still resemble sleeping guinea pigs.

Day 7

Some exceptionally precocious puppies begin to crawl around. At no other time does the sentence "To live is to grow" seem so true.

Day 7

Day 11: Eyes and ears begin to open.

Day 11

The nervous system is now developed enough to respond to external stimuli of light and sound; eyes and ears begin to open.

Day 14: Eyes and ears are now open.

Day 14

By now all the puppies should have opened eyes and ears. In some of them you may be able to feel the canine teeth through the gums. All puppies should crawl both forward and backward.

Day 16: Dogs, too, walk on wobbly legs at first.

Day 16

The puppies start to walk and stand on unsteady legs, trip over each other, and after a few steps collapse exhausted and fall instantly asleep. The litter looks much like a bunch of kids trying to ride their bicycles for the first time.

Day 18

The puppies now urinate and defecate on their own—in their box. The mother takes care of cleaning up and removing the feces.

Day 21

Now, at the age of three weeks, the socializing phase begins, a milestone in the development of a puppy. The siblings interact consciously with each other and begin to investigate their box. To some of them the box seems too confining, and they begin to try to leave the safe nest in order to explore the wider world. All of them can now navigate quite well, but they still fall down quite a lot when they try to run.

Week 4

The puppies are now able to carry toys around, tussle with each other, and pull on the shoelaces of visitors. They can eat soft solid food to supplement their mother's milk—if the mother still lets them at her teats. Fearless

Day 21

Weeks 3 and 4: Table manners are still an unknown concept.

Week 4: Nothing tastes as good as whatever Mother has just been eating.

Week 5: Gradually puppies turn into real dogs.

adventurers, they have long since stopped being content in their puppy box. The moment they start eating solid food the mother stops cleaning up after them.

Week 5

The puppies are growing fast now. Their movements become more and more coordinated, and their mental abilities keep developing. The puppies learn to recognize individual people and react to their voices. At the same time the mother starts training them, a process that should not be interfered with. Her disciplining them is very important for the later training of your puppy and for how it will accept your dominant position. If a puppy nips its mother too hard, punishment is swift and direct: a growl and a bite on the puppy's muzzle. The puppy is released as soon as it demonstrates its subordination. Then playing resumes as though nothing had happened; puppy experiences are never forgotten.

Week 6

The puppies have now learned the greeting ceremonials of grown ups and sniff each other's muzzle and anal region. Altogether they demonstrate more and more adult behavior. Patterns of submission and dominance are practiced within the group, and a hierarchy develops among the siblings. Social behavior is best practiced within the context of the litter. That is why it is much too early at this point in time to remove a puppy from the litter and take it home, no matter how cute it is. In the process of cavorting and fighting with its siblings the puppy learns how to behave with other dogs, how to play with them, when play gets too rough, when it is best to subordinate oneself, and what had better be taken seriously.

Weeks 6 and 7

Week 8

All the baby teeth should have grown in by now. During this week the puppies learn to be afraid. Although puppies are traditionally sold or given away at eight weeks, it's sometimes better for both you and your dog if you wait a week or two. A puppy that is petrified of riding in the car and perhaps even throws up will be frightened of car rides for a long time to come. If it is scared of anything else—dogs as well as humans tend to react with fear to

Week 8

Week 12: The puppy is no longer a baby but more like a young child.

is no longer a baby but comparable to a young child. It is capable of understanding the reasons for your reactions to what it does. Household rules should now be made clear. Don't allow the puppy to do anything that you won't want your full-grown dog to do. By now your dog will have the adult body temperature of 101.5° Fahrenheit (38.5° Celsius).

Week 16

At this age, most puppies begin to lose their baby teeth, starting usually with the incisors. From now on you should have rawhide bones handy at all times, or the legs of your kitchen table may never look the same again. New teeth growing in cause incredible itching—something you may have forgotten—and continual chewing and rubbing one's gums against semi-hard objects seems to offer the only relief. The puppy will now also start testing how seriously your "No's" and all your other rules and commands are to be taken. Obedience training is just as crucial at this point as

unfamiliar things—the object of its fear may evoke the same reaction for a long time. A traumatic experience at this stage can ruin all the socializing skills acquired thus far. One week is not a significant piece of your life, but it can make a huge difference in the life of your young dog. At ten weeks your puppy will be much more secure and stable and better able to start out on a new life.

Week 12

At this age the socializing phase is completed. Your dog

continued socialization. In this phase your teaching should rely mostly on positive reinforcement: Lots of praise, petting, and rewards will make your dog think lessons are fun. The world can seem like a scary and dangerous place or it can seem like a thrilling adventure. Your puppy's view of it is the mirror image of your own. Keep that in mind.

Sixth Month

Most of the internal organs are almost completely developed by now, but the skeleton is still growing. In fact, the bones are just beginning to become really solid. The puppy has a need for more calories now than a full-grown dog. At this stage, its body is only 63 percent water, and the heart has slowed to about 75 beats per minute. Toward the end of this month, all the permanent teeth should have grown in.

Week 16

At 6 months: How could anyone resist this look?

At 7 and 8 months: The peak of puberty, not the most pleasant age.

Months Seven and Eight

At about this age your dog enters puberty. If you thought that by getting your puppy housebroken you had cleared the greatest hurdle in the dog training process, you are in for a surprise. At seven to eight months, a dog is comparable to a thirteen- to fourteen-year-old teenager. This age period is not usually considered the most pleasant by parents. Your teenage dog may act as though it had never heard of words like "Sit," "Stay," "Heel," and "Come." It will test your dominant status and all the household rules just to see if they still hold. It may try to sit in your favorite armchair or have an "accident" on your bed pillow if you leave it at home alone. The command "No!" will evoke a surprised, non-comprehending expression. But don't despair. Your dog is behaving quite normally, and if you continue your training as before, all will turn out fine. After all, human teenagers, too, regain their sanity at one point or another.

The Search for a Dog

Where Will You Find the Dog of Your Dreams?

You can find dogs through the classified section of newspapers, in animal shelters, through ads in dog magazines, at dog shows, and even on street corners. You can also look on the Internet, and the various dog clubs will supply you with addresses of breeders.

If you have your heart set on getting a dog from an animal shelter, you are truly doing a good deed. Shelters are filled with tens of thousands of dogs in desperate need of a new home. Whether or not your story will have a happy ending will emerge in time.

The environmental and genetic influences that have shaped your dog are unknown, and you may therefore be in for many surprises—happy as well as unhappy ones. A dog with an unknown past needs to be handled with special patience, understanding, and tolerance. But if that does not faze you and you are willing to deal with whatever problems turn up, I congratulate you on your courage and wish you well. If you get a puppy, chances are relatively small that it has already suffered serious abuse from people.

Prepare yourself for your first visit to the shelter. Such visits are a nightmare for the soft-hearted. Harden your heart at least for a short time, or you will leave the shelter with every dog that howled or looked at you from its cage with especially sad eyes.

Keep reminding yourself what kind of a dog it is you want, what kind of personality. Pay as much attention to your head as to your heart. And listen to the staff of the shelter; let them tell you what they know about the dog that appeals to you. Tell them what kind of dog you are looking for and let them make suggestions. The cutest, most charming of all the dogs there may be the one that is hardest to live with.

People who sell puppies through newspaper ads may have let their dog get pregnant because they thought their bitch "should have a litter before she gets spayed" or because all their neighbors and friends told them Molly was simply the greatest dog and they would like to have one just like her; or perhaps Molly decided on her own to become a mother.

Most amateur breeders of this kind are ignorant about hereditary diseases, genetic factors, and other such subjects. If the puppies they sell are purebred, they are usually much cheaper than puppies from "real" breeders. But they are usually given away very early—too early—so that the owner will not have to bother with them any longer than necessary.

The Search for a Dog

Jack Russell Terriers

Raising puppies is expensive and time-consuming. It takes time and some adjusting to manage five, six, or more puppies, to treat them with love, and to keep them from ruining everything in your house. And the bigger they get the more supervision and care they require.

Even with so-called breeders it is important to be able to tell the good ones from the not so good ones. Responsible breeders let their bitch get pregnant only if they are reasonably sure— and that takes a certain

amount of experience—that there will be enough homes for the puppies. They have years of experience with dogs and the breed they raise. They care deeply about the mother of the puppies not just for sentimental or financial reasons but because she comes from a good line and is herself the result of responsible breeding. The stud dog is selected according to certain criteria, such as physical health, freedom from hereditary diseases, and excellent appearance and/or performance.

Good breeders treat their bitch and her puppies like royalty; the dogs get the most nutritious food, the best medical care, and all the attention they need. Breeders do this because they know their reputation depends on it. If they are neglectful in any one area it will show up in the puppies, and word will get around. The world of official dog breeding is small. Good health, physical beauty, and the ability to perform can't be achieved by pinching pennies.

If you are looking for a breeder, call the American Kennel Club (AKC) in New York City or get in touch with various other dog associations. These organizations will be able to steer you to specific breed clubs, which will in turn be able to tell you which breeder (as near you as possible) has or is expecting to have a litter. Talk to veterinarians. If possible, have a look at several litters and be as objective as you can. It doesn't matter where and from whom you get a dog as long as it is the dog that suits you best.

Good Breeders and Bad Breeders

Once you have decided on getting a puppy from a breeder there are several ways of locating a breeder of the kind of dog you want:
◆ From the AKC you may obtain the phone number and/or address of the breed club you are interested in. A breed club will be able to give you a list of breeders in your vicinity who either have or expect to have puppies. These clubs will be happy to send you informational brochures about the breed they represent. Most of these brochures include the breed standard along with assertions such as "these dogs are friendly, affectionate, and love children." They never tell you whether the breed is nervous, tends to develop hip dysplasia, or sheds loads of hair in the spring. Questions of this sort have to be put to the breeder or another knowledgeable person.

The AKC is advisory, and supplies information about and participates in many worthwhile canine projects. The AKC is a purebred dog registry and has no regulatory function other than enforcement of its registry, show, and exhibition rules. An AKC registered pup isn't guaranteed by that organization. AKC registration in no way assures the health, breeding, or showing value of parents of registered puppies; neither does the AKC certify or assure registered pups' good health or freedom from physical or hereditary diseases. Of course, even the AKC can't promise you that a given breeder treats his or her dogs really "well" or the way you think they should be treated.

You have to look into that yourself.

◆ Dog club magazines and breed publications list addresses of breeders, and many breed references may be obtained over the Internet. Some more recently introduced breeds are not registered with the AKC, and on the Internet you may find references to registry with the United Kennel Club (UKC), Continental Kennel Club, or other national breed clubs. To find the best breeder, visit several kennels and choose for yourself.

◆ Local newspapers often have a pet section, usually in the advertising supplement of their weekend editions, and some breeders put their ads in these papers. Once again, it is your job to find out which of the breeders are any good.

◆ Some sporting magazines carry advertisements by hunting-dog breeders who have puppies and sometimes older or trained dogs available. Some of these breeders can, however, be rather fussy and condescending if you, as a non-hunter, approach them with the desire to purchase one of their superbly trained hunting dogs.

◆ Dog shows. Would you like to see hundreds of breeders all in one place? Then go to a

Rhodesian Ridgebacks

dog show. First of all, you'll find it a most interesting experience (part of the fun is simply to observe some of the amazing excesses of human love for animals) and one that is particularly useful if you are still vacillating between two breeds. Nowhere else will you see so many first-rate representatives of the breeds you have narrowed your choice to. Secondly, you will have a chance to talk with owners and breeders and observe their dogs.

Call the AKC to find out the dates of major upcoming dog shows. Then try to get there as soon as the show opens. Buy a catalog, which will list the breeders of the breed you are interested in, the number of dogs shown, the numbers of the show rings, and the times when the dogs are judged. If you see anyone with a dog of your breed, start a conversation. Don't be shy. People who exhibit their dogs like nothing better than to talk about their dogs and sing the breed's praises. (This is true in everyday life as well. Anyone who is walking with a dog on the leash is approachable. Even I, who live in a big city with all the dangers of city streets, respond with a relaxed smile to any question about my dogs.) But keep in mind that in such conversations you get the opinion of only one person. If this person tells you that his Borzoi loves people and is extremely sociable, remember that this must be a very unusual Borzoi. Don't run out to get one for yourself, hoping that you will get an equally unusual representative of the breed. There are exceptions to every rule. Still, don't rely on the experience of one individual, whether positive or negative, when you pick a breed. Make the most of your day at the dog show; talk to different breeders, watch their dogs, and perhaps note a few telephone numbers. The names and addresses of all exhibitors are in the show catalog.

Most breeders will not try to talk you into buying one of their dogs. Don't be swayed by a breeder's glowing description of her dogs, and above all don't let anyone talk you into getting a breed your research has led you to eliminate because it is wrong for your situation. If a breeder tries to sell you a dog without questions, beware! This is not the right time yet for you to buy a dog anyway.

How to Tell a Good Breeder from a Bad One

Surely you don't want to get the puppy you have been looking forward to for so long, the dog you have thought about so much and whose breed characteristics you have analyzed in such detail from just any breeder. It's much better to seek out a responsible person with whom you can establish an honest relationship. Wouldn't it be nice if we could select our parents-in-law with the same care? Unfortunately, breeders do not state in their ads how seriously they take their responsibilities. Besides, many miserable breeders believe quite honestly that they are doing a great job. That is why you have to have some of a detective's skills to be able to tell a good

breeder from one who cuts corners. A detective has to ask questions, or she'll never find out the answers she's looking for.

A trustworthy breeder won't mind answering your questions to the best of his abilities because he will want

Bolognese

to ask you about things in your private life you'd be reluctant to tell your best friend about, let alone a stranger. Questions like how much you travel, what your typical day looks like, if you go out in the evening a lot, whether you do a lot of sports or would rather spend the weekend lounging in bed, and so on. The breeder is simply trying to find the best possible home for the dogs he has raised with such painstaking care, and for this he has to know quite a bit about you. A good breeder doesn't try to talk you into buying his dogs, and he won't sell you one at a bargain price because it's the only one left or because he is about to leave on vacation.

(I recently saw an ad in the paper that read "For sale: DALMATIAN puppies w/ papers; price reduced because of imminent relocation; ready to go now." Everything in this ad made me suspicious. Gestation in dogs lasts about 63 days. Had the breeder no idea three months previous that she might be moving? "Ready to go now" means that the breeder isn't particularly concerned about where the puppies will go as long as she is rid of them soon. "Price reduced" because of relocation—the clincher; stay away!)

After a breeder has told you over the phone whether or not he has or expects to have puppies and if the answer is yes, you should ask the following questions:
◆ Do you also have other breeds? (More than two breeds is always a warning sign. No one can take care of more than two breeds the way that the dogs deserve and that is good for the puppies.)
◆ At what age can one pick up the puppies? (If the answer is less than eight weeks, there is no point in going on. Thank her for her time, hang up, and dial the next number on your list.)
◆ How many dogs do you have? (As a rule, stay away from breeders that have too many dogs. More than fifteen is reason to be suspicious. No one can do justice to this many animals. Even if the dogs are in good health, they are often not as well socialized as dogs raised in smaller groups.)
◆ Do you keep your dogs in your home? (Watch out if the dogs are kept "mostly outdoors." These dogs have no chance to become accustomed to sounds like the clatter of pots, kids screaming, or folk music and to develop an immunity to them.)
◆ Can I see the puppies' mother when I come to visit? (If the answer is no, you have wasted your time. Dial the next breeder on your list. You have to see the mother in order to know what the puppies will look like. It's as simple as that. A breeder who is unwilling to let you see the puppies' mother is trying to hide something and will not do.)

A breeder might suggest that you look at one or more somewhat older puppies from a previous litter. Generally eight to ten weeks is the ideal age for puppies to leave their mother, but a somewhat older dog usually adjusts just as well to a new home if it has grown up in the breeder's home and is used to human family life. You should say no to young dogs five to nine months old that have grown up in a kennel. The transition from kennel life

to family life can be time-consuming and nerve-racking for you if your new dog is unacquainted with the sounds of a TV, cars, children's music tapes, and other noises and situations.

Advantages of a Young Puppy

Such a puppy comes to you with literally a blank slate. It has developed no bad habits yet. It will grow up

Shih Tzu

with you, and you will have a chance to train it from the beginning—and make your own mistakes.

Disadvantages of a Young Puppy

For several weeks or months, until it is housebroken, your puppy will demand a great deal of time and attention. It is still a baby when it arrives and therefore has to be treated very gently. It also

still needs peace and quiet and plenty of sleep. And you can't tell with 100 percent certainty how its personality will develop.

Advantages of an Older Puppy (4–5 Months)

Such a dog is emotionally more mature than a very young puppy and thus more can be asked of it. The daily routine doesn't have to be quite so rigorously structured. A dog this age is easier to play with and take out for walks. Perhaps it is already housebroken and familiar with the rules of normal family life. You can also tell better how its personality is likely to develop.

Disadvantages of an Older Puppy

Such a dog has seen more of life and may have formed its own opinions concerning certain methods of training or figured out ways of getting around them. Like a half-grown child, it might become rebellious and insolent as it undergoes various stages of physical development, and you may need more time to

Mastiffs

assert yourself as the alpha member of the pack.

If you have been favorably impressed by your first contact with a breeder, you should set up a date for a visit. This will be the time for in-depth questioning.

At the Breeder's

When you arrive at the breeder's place and see a big kennel containing a number of different kinds of dogs, get right back into your car and drive home, *no matter how clean and neat it may look*. You want a dog that was raised indoors, and you are looking for a breeder who gives her full attention to the breed you are interested in and to the dogs and puppies in her care; you don't want

an entrepreneur or mass producer.

The setup may be plain and show wear, but the dogs' surroundings must be absolutely clean. (With a whole litter of tiny puppies it is of course almost impossible to keep the floor entirely free of puddles and feces, but these should not look as though they have been there for hours.) The water bowls should be clean and full, and the food dishes should contain no old food, let alone ants. There should be no bottles, tin cans, or broken glass lying around in the dogs' outdoor area. The fencing should be strong and of reasonable height, without sharp edges or nails sticking out. It will be obvious that dogs live here, and the house and yard will bear the marks of their presence, but you should at least get the impression that someone is trying to keep things shipshape.

If, on the other hand, a breeder's house and yard show practically no evidence of dogs, if the floors are covered with light-colored wall-to-wall carpeting and you see no chewed-on toys anywhere, then there is reason to suspect that the dogs are not, contrary to assertions, kept in the house and yard but live somewhere in the cellar or in kennels way back on the property.

Watch for the Following Signs:

◆ Do the dogs—including the adult ones—look healthy?

◆ Do all the dogs respond affectionately and happily to the breeder?

◆ Are the grown dogs friendly toward you?

◆ Does the breeder seem to be knowledgeable about the breed?

◆ Is the breeder interested in why you chose this breed and in how you intend to keep your dog, and does he take the time to show you all his dogs?

◆ Does the breeder want to find out as much as possible about you? (Not who your friends are or what your favorite drink is but things that suggest what the future life of his puppy will look like.)

◆ Does the breeder seem proud of her puppies? And, even more important, does she seem to love them?

◆ If for some reason things did not work out, would you give your puppy back to this person? (If not, terminate your interview. You have to be able to establish a good relationship with the breeder of your puppy. If you don't have the sense that your puppy would have at least as good a life at the breeder's as with you, leave now—without the dog. Buying out of pity is a mistake.)

Now you have to start a whole barrage of questions. A breeder who is unwilling to answer questions or is made nervous by them is not worth your time. You are about to acquire a friend that will stick by you through thick and thin—a dog—and this requires some research. A good breeder will be pleased that you take the matter so seriously.

Ask the Following:

◆ How long have you been raising this breed? (Preferably for many, many years.)

◆ How many litters do you have a year? ("Many" is in this case the wrong answer.)

◆ What do you think are potential problems of this breed? (If the answer is "None" don't believe it.)

◆ Are there some things you watch out for particularly when you breed your dogs?

◆ How often do you have your dogs checked by the veterinarian? Have the sire and the dam been checked or X-rayed for hip dysplasia?

◆ Do your dogs have any kind of hereditary defects?

◆ Do you test your dogs for personality?

◆ May I see the pedigree of the puppy and your sales contract?

◆ May I see the veterinarian's reports on this litter?

◆ What is the life expectancy of this breed? How long did the oldest dog of this breed you ever had live?

◆ If I should find that for some disastrous or unavoidable reason (the house burning down, divorce, transfer to Hawaii) I am unable to keep the dog, would you take it back to find it a new home? (Be wary of a breeder who says no. A good breeder should always care about finding the best possible home for her dogs.)

The breeder will, for his part, observe you very closely, watching how you behave with the dogs and how the dogs react to you. He'll have quite a few questions of his own and probably ask you to stay in touch after you leave with the puppy. This is normal and a good idea. It doesn't mean that you have to send him cards on his birthday and for Christmas or show up for tea every few months. It is simply a sign that the breeder is interested in his dogs' future well-being and willing to stand by with advice or practical help if you need it. And that is as it should be. You'll be amazed how many questions will come up in the first few weeks and months of living with a new dog. Be grateful if you can feel free to call the breeder.

Salukis

The Personalities of Puppies

The Difficulty of Choosing

Prepare yourself well mentally and emotionally before you go to look at a litter of puppies for the first time. Define clearly for yourself what kind of personality the dog you are going to share your life with should have. Because as soon as you set eyes on a bunch of irresistibly cute puppies you'll be utterly charmed, and objectivity and rational thought fly out the window. The only words that will come to your lips are something like "Oh, how adorable!" But that's all right. It happens to us all. Still, this is not the best emotional state in which to choose a close companion for the next fourteen years.

Let the breeder help you. She has known the puppies from the day they were born, has seen them every day in their different moods and developmental phases, and

should be able, after talking with you for a while, to pick a puppy that fits your needs. In every litter there are dominant puppies, solitary types, and relatively aggressive individuals, and your breeder will know exactly which puppy belongs to which category. The statement "The puppy picked us, not the other way round" sounds nice but is usually

heard from people who later have the greatest problems with their dog.

Male or Female?

This is a question eternally debated by dog owners, and there is no authoritative answer to it. Some people swear by males, and others wouldn't consider any dog

Eurasians

but a female—until they own their first male. On the whole, females are somewhat gentler, friendlier, more affectionate, and often less dominant than males. But they come into heat twice a year, and you will find it trying when all the male dogs from miles around congregate at your door step, howling and ready to accompany you and your female dog on every walk around the block. But there are ways to deal with estrus, either by giving hormone injections, which are, however, dangerous to the dog's health in the long run, or by spaying, an operation most veterinarians recommend because it also reduces the risk of mammary cancer by 90 percent.

Male dogs, unlike females, can be seized by sexual desire any time of the year. Some become so obsessed that they are almost impossible to control. No fence is high enough, no distance too great, no door strong enough to stop them. They howl all night, run away any chance they get, and sometimes even refuse to eat. Some male dogs fight with other males, but others give you nothing but pleasure. If you are smart, you will not pay too much attention to the question of gender but will simply look for the puppy whose personality you like best.

A Bundle of Energy or a More Sedate Type?

Ask yourself ahead of time whether you want a dog that will challenge you, one that is full of spunk and needs lots of exercise and things to keep it busy (even at those moments when you are short on time and have other things to worry about, when you have to go away, or when you are expecting your fifth child), or a less active dog that is satisfied with whatever exercise and entertainment program you offer but that might not be a good candidate for taking on bicycle tours and has little enthusiasm for playing Frisbee. Decide whether you want a star athlete or more of a couch potato, a silly clown or a more spiritual type, before you let yourself be captivated by the soulful eyes of a fuzzy puppy.

Needless to say, this decision is always based on

Bolognese

feelings. But rational criteria should not be neglected. Certain character traits are evident in puppies, behavior patterns that will persist into later life, such as fearfulness, inhibition, curiosity, wildness, delight in retrieving, and aggressiveness. People who train dogs for police work and for leading the blind, as well as hunters, use some tricks to determine a puppy's personality and stability of temperament. One such trick is to blow up a paper bag and then pop it above the puppies. A puppy that doesn't run to its mother or hide under the nearest sofa but instead comes to investigate the source of this interesting sound is clearly not very fearful and is unlikely to be gun-shy. (However, if it shows no reaction at all, it is most likely deaf.)

Of course, a breeder of Maltese puppies will probably show you the door the moment you start waving a heavy bunch of keys at the puppies or blowing up paper bags. There are other, less disruptive ways to find out about the emotional stability and certain character traits of a puppy. The best time for this is when the puppies are about seven to ten weeks old.

Start by watching the entire litter without interacting in any way yourself. You want to see how the puppies behave among themselves without being distracted by a strange human being. This is the only way to tell the temperament of each individual puppy. Ideally you should be able to visit the puppies several times, at different times of day, and preferably over a period of several days or a week. Puppies undergo such mind-boggling changes within a few days that you may have a hard time recognizing them after a few weeks.

So there they are, two or three or seven tiny fur balls with huge eyes and wagging tails. If, when you enter the room, six of the seven scurry away from you in terror, you can leave then and there. Even if the seventh puppy remained sitting, you can assume with 98 percent certainty that it is not the right dog for you. It may just be that its timidity gene has not yet swung into full action. But if the puppies don't run away, what do you do? Basically, the puppies should play together, tails pointing straight up and

Jack Russell Terriers

wagging happily, until they drop. When you look more closely, you'll see that the individual puppies already have different, clearly recognizable personalities. Which of them is strong, noisy, and a show-off? Which one is retiring, gentle, and ready to subordinate itself? Which ones win and which lose when they play tug-of-war? Most people do best with dogs that are neither the leader of the pack nor the Cinderella among the siblings. Look for the puppies that don't initiate play and fighting but are always ready to join in the fray and defend their position.

Recognizing an energetic dog is easy: It's the puppy that spends relatively little time sleeping and is in constant motion, playing with toys or a sibling, pouncing on its mother, or trying to climb out of the box in search of excitement and adventure. Telling an especially calm puppy is also not difficult: It's usually the one that sleeps the most, is not easily upset, and responds to anything new by first just watching. Occasionally you'll see a puppy in a litter that doesn't want to have much to do with its siblings and prefers to be by itself. These dogs often are not in very good health, suffering from respiratory or heart

The first lessons of pack hierarchy are learned through play. (Dalmatians)

problems that keep them from indulging in rough play, or else they are exceptionally independent. Later on, when living with people, these dogs tend to show the same aloofness toward their human masters and family. This works against bonding and makes training much more difficult because these dogs are too absorbed in their own world.

Don't fall, either, for the puppy that is the first one to come running up to you on wobbly legs. Chances are it would greet anyone else just as enthusiastically. It is probably the ringleader of the bunch, in other words, the alpha puppy. Depending on the breed, this may or may not present a problem. In so-called companion dogs or lap dogs it doesn't matter so much, but with terriers or larger dogs it makes a big difference whether or not your dog keeps challenging you and testing your position of authority in the family. You'll recognize the alpha puppy because it keeps taking toys away from the others, is at the center of any tussle, gets to the food dish first, and is most likely to

turn play into serious business.

Also stay away from a puppy that is reluctant to join the fray of its siblings, is afraid of new toys, and backs away timidly from you or—worse—from its owner. Don't try to convince a shy puppy to be more courageous, and don't imagine that you'll succeed in "freeing the little fellow of his inhibitions."

You don't know the

puppy's genetic disposition or what is going on in its little brain. Timid puppies often turn into timid dogs that snap at anything that scares them, such as a running child or an adult on roller blades. Maybe at some point in the future you can adopt a timid dog as a kind of rehabilitation project, but wait until you have more experience with dogs.

After you have observed the litter for a while, you can

Every pants leg and every shoelace represents a new adventure.

start drawing attention to yourself. Clap your hands lightly, snap your fingers, rattle your keys, whistle softly. Normal puppies will be utterly intrigued by these unusual sounds and this unfamiliar pair of legs. They'll sit on your shoes, try to climb up on you, pull your shoe laces, and nibble on your fingers. Which puppies react to the sounds you make? Which come up to you to have a closer look? Which act scared and timid?

Most people are happiest with a dog that is attentive and curious. A nervous dog has a hard time coping with the normal daily life of our modern world and might grow into a hysterical one-hundred-pound creature that doesn't like to go outside and has to be dragged through the neighborhood against its will. A puppy that pays no attention at all is too insensitive or independent. If all the puppies seem sleepy or uninterested, ask the breeder if they have just eaten or if they have been playing to exhaustion. Some puppies simply keel over and are instantly asleep after playing wildly a minute

before; others sit down and nod off gradually, a little like some elderly gentlemen at the opera. Their sleeping is no reason for worry; puppies, like children, need their sleep.

Personality Test for Puppies

Now ask if you may look at the puppies individually and do some simple personality testing. Ask to see them one at a time in another room or a fenced outdoor area, a place, preferably, that the puppy is not so familiar with. The breeder or your family may be present at these tests as long as they don't distract the puppy or play with it.

This test, too, is best done when the puppies are seven to ten weeks old.

Interest in Humans

The puppy should be placed on the floor in surroundings that are new to it. Step away a few paces and crouch down. Then call the puppy in a cheerful, encouraging tone, clap your hands, or pat the ground next to you.

Normal: The puppy comes toward you immediately with tail up in the air and a happy expression on its face.

Dominant: The puppy dashes up to you immediately, leaps up on you, and nips at your hands or clothes.

Subordinate/timid: The puppy approaches hesitantly and with an expression of uncertainty, ears somewhat flattened.

Independent: Instead of coming up to you, the puppy first investigates the surroundings.

Following

Get up and move away from the puppy. Don't ask it to follow you. Watch its reaction.

Dominant: The puppy follows you instantly with pricked ears and chases your feet.

Normal: The puppy follows you with pricked ears and stays very close to you.

Subordinate/timid: The puppy follows hesitantly, with drooping tail and an

Crouch down; the puppy should come up to you instantly.

expression of uncertainly. It might move in a crouching position or even crawl.

Independent: The puppy wanders off in some other direction instead of following you.

Interest in Retrieving

Crumple some paper up into a ball, and when the puppy has noticed it, throw it a few paces ahead of the puppy.

Dominant: The puppy runs after the crumpled paper, brings it back, dodges your reach, and refuses to let go of the paper or perhaps even growls.

Ideal: The puppy chases after the paper instantly, brings it back, and lets you take it away.

Normal: The puppy gets hold of the paper, carries it off somewhere and starts

The puppy should follow you with perked ears.

chewing on it but lets you take it away without protest.

Subordinate/timid: The puppy acts nervous or uncertain when the paper ball rolls past it, runs after it hesitantly, or doesn't dare approach it when it stops rolling.

Independent: The puppy shows no interest in the paper at all.

Dominance Behavior I

Take the puppy in your lap or hold it down on the floor in front of you; roll it on its side and then the back. Keep it in this position until it relaxes.

Dominant/independent: The puppy struggles to get out of this position and tries with all its might to turn right side up, attempts to bite your hands, and complains.

Normal: The puppy struggles at first but then calms down.

Subordinate/timid: The puppy doesn't struggle at all, staying on its back passively and perhaps even licking your hands.

Dominance Behavior II

Pet the puppy, stroking its head, neck, shoulders, and back. Touch its ears, muzzle, and paws. Rub it vigorously with both hands, almost as though you were rubbing it dry with a towel.

Dominant: The puppy struggles to get free, jumps up on you, gets very excited, and snaps or growls.

Normal: The puppy squirms with pleasure or plays gently with you.

The urge to retrieve is instinctive—relinquishing the prey is not.

Subordinate/timid: The puppy immediately turns on its back, presenting its belly.

Independent: The puppy struggles to get free and walks away.

Evaluating the Puppy

After you have run through all the tests, add up the "normals," "dominants," "timids," and "independents." Most people, and especially families with children, will be happiest with a dog that scores at least three or four "normals." A puppy that gets three or four "dominant" or "independent" marks will need a very firm hand and very thorough obedience training. Depending on the breed, it might develop into an aggressive and belligerent dog. A puppy that was judged "subordinate/timid" three or four times has to be trained very carefully and gently, which can sometimes be just as difficult as training a dominant dog. In the case of some breeds, a very timid, hesitant, or nervous puppy can turn into a timid adult that may bite out of fear when it is frightened. A puppy that is a "mixed bag" with the evaluations running

The puppy should soon learn to put up with lying on its back.

all over the map is too difficult to "read." Its reaction to obedience training and to unforeseen situations are quite unpredictable, and such a dog can't therefore be recommended to a first-time owner.

Note of caution: Always keep in mind what breed the puppies you are observing belong to. If it is a breed with a gentle and subordinate character, most puppies will react in a restrained, docile manner; whereas if you are testing a dominant "daredevil" breed, most of the puppies will respond true to type. Such uniformity of reaction is an indication that the majority of the litter will develop the traits—dominance, independence, or restraint— typical of the breed, and this speaks well for the breeder. It also makes the choice much easier for the buyer. Still, especially in the case of dominant breeds, most people do best with dogs that are more in the range of "normal."

If none of the puppies appeals to you, tell the breeder politely that although the puppies are very nice, none of them is exactly what you are looking for. You'll no doubt feel disappointed, but you'd be much worse off if you were to take the wrong puppy. Call the next breeder on the list. Take your time. Your patience will pay off.

Eurasians

How About One More?

There you are, surrounded by the cutest little puppies. After all the tests and extensive discussions with the breeder, the choice has narrowed down to two. They are playing together beautifully and the breeder is telling you that these two are inseparable.

Shouldn't you in such a case take both? They'd be happy being together. There'd always be someone to play with, and the pain of separation from the mother and the rest of the litter

Signs of Health in Puppies

If you have come to look at a litter of puppies, observe the following indicators of good health:

◆ A puppy's bright, shiny eyes may make you fall in love with the dog, but that is not the point. They are a sign of good health and a happy spirit. A small amount of clear discharge is normal, but a colored discharge from the eyes can indicate inflammation. If the skin around the eyes is bare, the puppy probably has mites.

◆ A black secretion from the ears with a penetrating odor indicates an ear infection and possibly mites.

◆ A round little belly is normal and desirable in puppies; the ribs should not be visible, but a bloated belly suggests worms. A bloated belly is not to be confused with the full belly all puppies have after they have been eating.

◆ The fattest puppy is not necessarily the healthiest. With puppies that will grow into big dogs, the opposite often holds. Every excess gram of fat in the growth period weighs on the still tender joints and can give rise to degenerative changes (e.g., joint problems).

◆ The coat of a healthy, well cared for puppy is clean, soft, and silky. A puppy that has just been wrestling with its siblings or stomped through the food dish may not look very presentable, but you should still be able to tell if it has a healthy coat. If a puppy doesn't look very clean, watch for the following: Is the little furry mop playful and full of energy or apathetic and withdrawn? If you spot tiny black dots in the fur, these are flea feces, and you can assume with certainty that the entire litter has fleas (and consequently worms as well).

◆ With males, check if you can feel both testicles. (Don't be embarrassed, nobody will mind; this is something like a building inspection. If you don't want to do it or don't know what to feel for, ask the breeder to do it.) If only one testicle has descended and the other is stuck in the abdominal cavity, the dog will need surgery later to correct this and prevent possible tumors.

◆ A healthy puppy should have a cool, moist nose, though after wild play or on warm days the nose may sometimes feel dry. If the nose is runny or if mucus comes from the nostrils, the puppy is sick. The gums should be pink, not red or pale to whitish. The teeth must be white.

would be minimized. Of course you'd love to take them all. And in the case of some dogs, keeping several is no problem at all and may even be a good idea.

However, if this is your first dog you are much better off getting used to the dog-keeping routine with just one animal. For a novice, getting even one puppy housebroken can be a challenge; with two, you have to pay twice the attention and keep an eye on two dogs at once. Getting two puppies at the same time multiplies not just the joys but also the difficulties. It is harder training two puppies at once because they are less focused on "their" human being; they are a pack and always have each other to follow, especially if one of them has just had a better idea than to *Sit!* The command *Come!* also is hard to obey when your sibling looks as though it had just seen something enormously exciting off in the other direction. Even with grown dogs the pack syndrome can be a problem. If a pair are male and female, the male will probably be busy most of

the time defending the female against other males, which does not make for peaceful and relaxed walks. Even if the two are of the same sex, the same situation can still arise, with the dominant dog taking on the defender role. Or the dominant one may not allow its companion to play with other dogs.

Training two young dogs simultaneously is no longer a relatively simple matter but amounts to a major undertaking, and one that an ordinary dog owner may hardly be up to. What would you do, for example, if you were trying to teach your dogs to *Heel!* and all they had on their little minds was chewing on the leash and each other's ears? When training dogs, you should always be dealing with just one of them and keep the others out of sight. This in itself is not easy if you have several dogs because, after all, most people have no more than twenty-four hours a day.

Dogs with a hunting instinct present an additional problem. If one dog comes upon a scent, the other or

others will undoubtedly be off in a flash along with the first one. That is the way dogs find out how much fun it is to hunt as a pack and perhaps to chase game. From that moment on you won't ever be able to walk them anymore without a leash. A highly energetic and smart dog can think up all kinds of trouble; if two of them put their heads together you haven't got a chance.

With less active breeds or companion dogs, keeping several usually presents no problem. (Although, keeping two or more Yorkshire Terriers, dogs that are not aware that they have been classified as companion dogs and still think of themselves as rat catchers and defenders of the city of York, is not altogether peaceful.)

Pugs, on the other hand, are better kept in pairs. Maltese and Italian Grey-hounds, too, can be kept in multiples without problem. But it is best to bring home one puppy to start with and to get a second one only when the first is six to eight months old and has mastered basic obedience

lessons. By that time it understands what the command *Come!* means and that urinating indoors is a no-no. By then you will also be able to judge better whether or not a second dog is a good idea.

Gordon Setters

Arrival at Home

The moment when you'll finally have a dog is almost here, but there are still a few things you have to do before you go to pick up your puppy.

Decide where your dog's **sleeping place** is to be. The best spot is a quiet corner free of drafts in the room where most of the family's activities take place so that your dog will be able to keep you and the other members of the household in sight. In most cases this will be the kitchen. For the first few nights, and as long as your puppy is not yet house-broken, you should keep next to your bed a **cardboard box** lined with towels and tall enough so the puppy can't climb out. Then when the puppy is afraid in the night and starts whining you can simply reach your hand into the box without having to get up. If the puppy gets restless because it has to relieve itself, the noise will wake you up and you can take the little fellow out right away, which you can't do if he is sleeping off in the hall and proceeds to make his puddle there in another corner. And believe me, during the first nights you won't sleep much anyway because you'll be so excited.

Keep a **hot-water bottle** handy, along with a ticking alarm clock. If your puppy gets terribly lonely at night you can stick these accessories under its blanket and simulate maternal warmth and the heartbeat of siblings.

An old **playpen** is a wonderful substitute for a kennel for the times when you have to leave the house briefly or want to work in peace without having to keep

Chow Chows

an eye on a bored puppy that is on the lookout for excitement and adventure. Put a blanket or pillow in the pen to serve as a bed, a few toys, a rawhide bone, and a dish of water. Then you won't have to worry, and your puppy will learn that every once in a while it is not the center of the universe.

Shopping List

Before your new family member moves in, you'll have to go shopping. Dog food is, of course, the most important item because, as we all know, the way to a dog's heart is through its stomach. You'll start life together on a better footing if the puppy doesn't throw up food that doesn't agree with it and doesn't have an attack of diarrhea on your Persian rug the first day. Call the breeder and ask what brand of dog food he's been using and get the same kind. If you don't like it you can gradually, over the next few weeks, change over to a different brand. After all, you don't want to complicate the huge adjustments the

puppy has to deal with by adding digestive problems like tummy aches and diarrhea.

You'll need food and water dishes that won't tip over or slide on the floor. There are dishes of stainless steel and of heavy, practically unbreakable stoneware that can't be chewed and are easy to clean. You may want two water dishes, one to put in the kitchen and one for outdoors.

Your new pet will also need a place it can claim as its own because every dog, just like every human, needs a place to retreat to when things are overwhelming. Here no limits are set to your imagination; the industry catering to canine needs has thought of just about everything from plastic and willow baskets in all conceivable shapes to soft and puffy pillows that are usually round or rectangular but can be patterned after sofas or beds for people—anything the heart desires, especially the human heart, is available. Dogs, of course, couldn't care less about what their retreat looks like as long as it is in a draft-free

corner, allows for watching the human goings-on, and is made comfortable with old blankets or pillows. It is almost always a good idea to have a dog bed in the kitchen (in most families that is the center of domestic activities) and one in the room where the family spends most of its time (the living room, or the study?). Your dog will always want to be where you are.

You'll also want a collar and a leash—at first a small collar suitable for a puppy and a lightweight leash, and later an adult collar appropriate for the size of the dog and a heavier leash.

In addition you'll want a plastic identification tag, like those used on luggage, or, better yet, an engraved metal tag, which you can usually get made at a hardware store. The information on the tag should include your phone number and address and perhaps your name and your dog's name. Attach the tag to the collar right away. Almost all dogs get lost at some point or another, and you will get your pet back much more quickly if your phone number is included on the tag.

French Bulldog

Toys are essential because if you don't get any for your dog, the dog will take care of the matter on its own. It may take a special fancy to your favorite shoes or the teddy bear your children like to sleep with or the fringes of your most expensive carpet. Take it from me, the dog will find something. So make life easier for both your dog and yourself and buy a few items: rawhide bones to satisfy its need for chewing, light-weight rubber balls (the heavy ones hurt if they bounce off the puppy's nose), and some squeaky squeeze toys. Make sure there are no buttons, eyes, or other embellishments that could come off and that your dog might swallow. (As a rule you can give your dog anything you would give a small child.)

You will also need a brush. Rough-coated and wire-haired dogs need a wire

Every dog must have a place to retreat to (Longhaired Dachshund).

brush; long-haired ones, a comb, and short-haired ones need to be rubbed down with a nubbly glove. Then you have to have dog shampoo (canine skin has a different pH level than does human skin, which is why ordinary shampoo is not good for dogs), tick tweezers, and a small pair of blunt-tipped scissors to be able, if necessary, to cut the hair away from a wound, around the anus, or around the eyes.

If you plan to take your dog along on trips, you'll need some travel equipment, such as a blanket or a bed that can be rolled up, a spill-proof water bottle for long car trips, and a small food dish. Dried food is easiest on trips. You should also pack the dog's favorite toy, the immunization record, perhaps a muzzle (required in some places, notably European countries, and a good thing to have along just in case), and a retractable leash. In strange cities and on parking lots dogs usually can't run free, and a retractable leash allows them at least some freedom of movement.

Basic Equipment for a Dog
- food dish
- water dish
- collar
- leash
- address tag
- dog basket
- toys
- brush

Travel Kit for a Dog
- collar and retractable leash
- food and water dishes
- blanket
- a toy
- dry food
- water bottle
- vaccination certificate
- possibly a muzzle

German Shepherd

Ten Tips for Traveling with Dogs

1 Make your reservations early. If you are going to travel by air, you will have to say when you make your reservation that you want to fly with your dog in the cabin. Airline rules vary, so be sure to check when you make your flight reservations. All states have quarantine regulations; ask your veterinarian to look them up for you. Health certificates are required for interstate and international travel. Hotels and campgrounds all have individual requirements; again, ask about them when making reservations.

2 If your dog is going to be traveling in the airplane's baggage compartment, plan the trip so that it will involve as little stress for your dog as possible. Book direct flights to minimize the time your dog will be left in its crate. In the summer, try to fly in the evening (when it's cooler), and in the winter, during the day (when it's warmer).

3 Take your dog to the veterinarian for a check-up before any long trip. A healthy dog is a happy dog; and it is no fun trying to find a veterinarian in a strange city, especially if you don't know the language. (Even if you do, would you know how to say "urinary tract infection" in Portuguese?)

4 If you plan to travel abroad, check first to see whether dogs are allowed in the country you want to visit (England and Australia are out because they require a quarantine period of six months) and what health certificates and immunizations are required.

5 Make sure your dog wears a tag on its collar with your address and telephone number. It is also a good idea to include your name and the phone number where you will be staying. A colorful key ring works best for this purpose. It's not particularly elegant, but it is practical.

6 Give your dog a light meal and plenty of water a few hours before leaving to prevent it from throwing up or getting diarrhea out of sheer excitement (a major problem when traveling by air, as I can tell you from personal experience). Take a long walk before you set out on the trip (whether by car or plane), so the dog is relaxed and won't suddenly have to relieve itself.

7 For long car trips you should use a seat belt designed for dogs or have the dog ride in the back section of the car separated from the front by a net or wire grate. (It's no fun if your dog

suddenly starts jumping around in the car and pulling on your sleeve because it feels like playing.) For airline flights, supply drinking water in a spill-proof container. For travel in the cargo section you can get flight crates of standard sizes at pet stores or from airline companies.

8 Make things as comfortable as possible for your dog in the back of the car or the flight crate. Cover the bottom of the crate with newspapers and a thick towel. Ask baggage loaders to leave your dog's crate outside the cargo hatch until shortly before departure. A significant tip will usually assure that your wishes are complied with, and your dog may receive special handling as well. For short flights of just a few hours, a dog can do without water. For short trips by car, spread the dog's blanket in the back of the car and take along a water bottle and a small food dish.

9 The flight crate must never have a lock on it. The airline personnel must always be able to release the animal in an emergency.

10 Avoid using tranquilizers (for the dog, that is; whether you want to use them yourself is up to you). Tranquilizers can cause major fluctuations in the body temperature of dogs and can therefore be quite dangerous. If you have prepared your dog as suggested above, you should not have to resort to tranquilizers. If you decide to use them anyway, you and your veterinarian should test, before you set out on the trip, how the dog reacts to them. A mild and less risky sedative is available in the form of so-called "rescue remedy drops," a plant-based relaxant that you can get at pharmacies and that you can add to the dog's drinking water.

Coton de Tulear

Jack Russell Terriers

How to Dog-proof Your Home

Just as you have to take some precautions if there are small children in your home, you have to make some preparations if a young dog moves in with you. Puppies, like young children, are terribly curious, investigate everything, put things in their mouths, and chew on everything. Go through your house and garden and remove all possible dangers. Move breakable things out of reach, get cigarettes out of the way, and if your puppy is fair-sized don't leave any ashtrays on the coffee table. Nicotine poisoning is a serious danger. Store all

Dangers for Puppies

Kitchen and bathroom
◆ bones that may splinter
◆ toiletries
◆ cleaning agents
◆ pits of cherries, apricots, and peaches (they contain prussic acid)
◆ medications
◆ hairpins and hair clips

Living room and bedroom
◆ nylon stockings
◆ sewing needles
◆ electric cords
◆ cigarettes
◆ chocolate
◆ potted plants
◆ lit candles

Study and children's room
◆ paper clips
◆ electric cords
◆ scissors
◆ small toys
◆ glues

Yard and garage
◆ fertilizers
◆ plants treated with insecticides
◆ mouse and rat poison
◆ fish hooks
◆ slug poison
◆ antifreeze

cleaning agents, medications, and perfume where the dog can't get at them. Check that there are no paper clips, nails, or screws lying around. Paint all electrical cords with a bitter tasting substance you can buy at pet stores; that way your puppy won't get in the habit of chewing on these rubbery strips that feel so good in the mouth. Pick up any broken glass, tin cans, and pieces of plastic in your garden or yard. Lock away antifreeze, fertilizers, and rat poison. In the children's room make sure there are no toys whose eyes could be bitten off. Watch out for stray Lego pieces and for Barbie dolls whose heads could be chewed off. Think of how your children would feel if they found a decapitated Barbie!

All this does not mean that you have to declare a state of emergency or that you have to blacktop your yard. It may sound to you as if you have to watch out like a hawk all the time, but in reality there are just a few things to keep in mind, and soon safety measures will become habit.

Bull Terriers

Fetching the Puppy

When you pick up your dog, ask for its immunization record, and, in the case of a purebred dog, its pedigree papers. A written sales agreement should include the breeder's name, the name of the kennel, the address of the buyer, and the price paid. Also: date of birth, name, and sex of the puppy, its stud book number, and a veterinarian's certi-fication that the puppy has no discernable congenital conditions, and is free from contagious diseases.

And now the big moment has come: You are finally handed your dog. Keep in mind, though, that wonder-ful and exciting as this moment may be for you, it may be quite frightening for the puppy. Up to now it has lived in a small world of familiar smells, the warmth of siblings, and the strict but loving presence of its hairy mother. Nothing it is about to experience will be familiar; everything will be new and a great adventure. Try to make this adventure as untraumatic as possible. There should be at least two of you driving home. While one person drives, the other holds the puppy on his or her lap or in a small basket lined with thick layers of newspaper and talks to it. It is practically impossible to calm a puppy, control one's own excitement, and drive all at the same time without ending up in the nearest ditch. Have some paper towels handy in case

On the way home, don't allow the puppy to roam the back seat freely. He should ride in a cardboard box or on the lap of a passenger.

nervousness or motion sickness makes the puppy vomit. If the puppy is very agitated, you may want to stop after ten or fifteen minutes at an appropriate spot and play with it for a while. The first car trips will determine whether or not your dog will love riding in the car for the rest of its life or whether it will be a nervous wreck every time it has to get into a car. So take your time.

Drive straight home without detours or stops along the way, and keep the welcome-home party as small as possible. If all your friends and relatives want to meet the puppy, plan the party for a later time. Don't overwhelm your puppy. If your children are all excited about the puppy's arrival, tell them beforehand to be as quiet and restrained as possible because a puppy is easily frightened. Nor should they fight over who will be the first to pick it up. After all, the puppy is not going away and everyone will have plenty of opportunity to snuggle with the dog. The animal will be in a state of mild shock because it has

just been torn away from all its family, including all the humans it has known. Right now it has to find out where it is and what its place is in this new world.

When you get home, take the puppy into the kitchen first, where it is warm and comfortable and where its sleeping basket, food, and water are ready waiting for it. Make yourself a cup of tea and watch the puppy explore its new quarters. If it acts fearful and insecure, sit down on the floor next to it and have your tea there. Let it decide where it wants to settle: on its bed, in your lap, or under a chair. If it wants to play, play with it but wait until it makes the first move. Don't wave all the new toys in front of its nose. Keep its new world as quiet and small as possible to start with. The more secure the puppy feels, the sooner it will venture farther afield.

If it starts sniffing the floor intently and circling with rounded back, swoop it up and take it to a place in the yard where you want it to relieve itself in the future. Even though it may take some time at the beginning,

the puppy will soon understand what is expected of it in this spot. And let it sleep if it wants to. After all, it is still a baby.

If You Have Other Pets

Take your time introducing the puppy to other pets. If you have rabbits, hamsters, or other small cage animals you can wait until the puppy discovers them on its own. Depending on the size and emotional security of the rabbit (or whatever animal), you can simply pick it up in your arms and let the puppy see it without calling special attention to it. Show it to the puppy briefly and then continue doing whatever you were doing, holding the little beast on your arm. You may want to go on playing ball, which the dog will bring back to you and to the rabbit you are still holding. The more of a to-do you create, the more exciting the object in your arms will appear to the dog, and that is exactly what you want to avoid. Act as if the rabbit is as normal a part of your household as

your kids, the toys, and the vacuum cleaner.

If you have a cat that is used to being the spoiled ruler of the roost, you have to proceed with a little more cunning. Don't make any fuss when you first come home with the dog but take

about how this creature ended up here. Before all this you may want to rub some catnip into the puppy's fur (or have the person do so who is keeping the puppy company in the kitchen), and then proceed to the kitchen with the cat. Don't

consider it its social obligation to approach the cat on wobbly feet, an act of politeness not likely to be well received. Let your cat hiss and spit all it wants; just talk to it and tell it that it is your favorite pet and will remain number one.

The smell of catnip on the puppy is important during the first few days. Catnip acts like a mild narcotic on cats, making them roll in it and purr ecstatically. This herb—catnip causes no reaction in dogs, by the way, even if they eat it, which they do only because someone else's food always tastes better than one's own—contains a slightly hallucinogenic substance that evokes feelings of euphoria in cats. This is just what you want at a time when a new family member appears whom the cat will probably be less than fond of. Don't leave the cat and dog together unsupervised during the first weeks because the consequences for the naive little puppy would probably be unpleasant. However, if the cat swats the dog in your presence, don't scold it or

Love at first sight is rare in situations like this.

it to the kitchen where some other person can look after it while you go find the cat. Let the cat sniff your hands, which will undoubtedly smell of the strange puppy, and tell your cat that you are just as much in the dark

carry the cat; it will come on its own, and it should have somewhere to escape to in case it is seized by panic (which is most likely). The other person in the kitchen should keep a loose hold on the puppy, which might

bend over backwards to console the puppy. Your cat has reason to be angry at this intruder, and a swat to the head is no great tragedy. The less fuss made over it, the less it will seem to hurt.

Keep your puppy away from horses until it is at least five or six months old. That is still early enough for it to get use to these monstrously big animals. A very young puppy whose movements are not yet perfectly coordinated can't get out of a horse's way as quickly as it should, and its little paw could end up under the horse's hoof all too quickly—don't forget that a horse weighs about 500 kg. You can easily imagine the effects on a puppy's paw of being stepped on.

The First Night in the New Home

Be prepared not to get too much sleep the first night, and perhaps the next few. This is the first time in the puppy's life that it is not spending the night snuggled up to its siblings' bellies. Instead it finds itself in a world where everything is new and nothing smells or

Golden Retriever

sounds the way it should. Let the puppy sleep next to your bed the first few nights. (Be sure to find a permanent sleeping place outside your bedroom within a few days, though—read on!) Take the box your TV came in or any other suitable carton, and put the puppy's blanket in it. The carton has to be big enough so that the puppy can't climb out and has to wake you if it has to relieve itself during the night. Dogs normally don't mess their bed, and your puppy will therefore get restless and whine so that you can pick it

up and take it outside to its place. I can assure you, it is a lot more pleasant to hear a snoring, grunting little dog next to your bed than to listen all night to a desperately lonely and frightened dog howling in the kitchen.

Some puppies settle down in their new home at bedtime without protest and sleep through the night. If you are the owner of such a unique creature, congratulations! But if you have a homesick little creature, which is more likely, put a hot-water bottle and a ticking alarm clock

under its blanket or pillow to simulate the warmth and heartbeat of siblings. If the puppy gets restless and you are sure it has relieved itself recently enough, let one hand hang into the box so that the puppy knows it is not alone. That should help it calm down again.

Now ask yourself seriously if you want your dog to sleep next to your bed for the rest of its life. If you let it sleep there you will have peaceful nights, but you'll never be able to get it to sleep elsewhere. Once it has gotten used to the warmth and comfort of your bedroom it will be difficult to make it accept a lonely, cold spot in the hall.

If anything seems unusual or strange to you, call the breeder. Don't worry: She will want to know how your puppy is doing and will be happy to help you. The breeder is the best person to turn to; she knows everything about the dog's breed and about the difficulties new owners tend to run into. Besides, the privilege of asking dumb questions is included in the purchase price.

The puppy can't climb out of this box without letting you know.

Arrival at Home

Golden Retriever

Basset Hound

The First Weeks at Home

Now it is here, the little puppy we have dreamed of so long—and from now on life will never again be the same. Whether you were organized before or not, order and routine will now be the name of the game, at least as far as your daily activities with the young dog are concerned.

Keep to a strict daily regimen. Puppies (like children) need a fairly rigid structure to their day to feel secure. Any pattern your puppy can recognize (walk after breakfast; this box is for sleeping; at such and such a time there will be another meal; the small person coming home means it's time to play) increases its confidence and self-assurance.

The Daily Schedule of a Puppy

Make a schedule that allows you to continue living your own life around your puppy's needs to eat and sleep. At age three to six months, a puppy has to be fed three times a day; between six months and a year, twice a day.

◆ The puppy has to be taken out immediately after you get up (around 6:30 to 7 A.M.)

◆ Breakfast shortly thereafter (around 7:30 A.M.).

◆ Fifteen minutes after eating it has to go out again.

◆ Then it's time to play, either alone or with you, to be followed by a nap.

◆ The puppy has to go out every two or three hours. Also after every nap.

◆ Second feeding around noon.

◆ Fifteen minutes later the puppy has to relieve itself again.

◆ Then it's time to play and sleep again.

◆ The puppy has to go out again every two or three hours.

◆ Third feeding around 5 P.M.

◆ Fifteen minutes later...

◆ The puppy still has to go out every two to three hours, the last time just before you go to bed.

Didn't I tell you at the beginning that you'd get a healthy, ruddy complexion?

Don't give the puppy anything more to eat after its last meal. It's in your own interest. The emptier the little stomach and intestines, the less your night's rest will be disrupted. And you need strong nerves for the next few weeks.

Walks

Take it easy with your puppy at the beginning. Don't take it on long walks. There will

Great Dane

be plenty of time for that, but for now the young animal's bones and nerves must not be overtaxed. After it has received all its vaccinations, it can safely be walked outside your yard, but don't allow contact with other dogs yet. **Do not** for the time being take it to the nearest field where dogs congregate. You do, of course, want to socialize your puppy well and have is meet as many dogs as possible. Playing with other dogs is the best possible exercise for it, but for now the young animal has enough to cope with getting used to you, your family, and the way

you function. There is no need to confront it now with unfamiliar dogs, their moods, and their ideas of play. Keep your puppy's world small and manageable for now. If you know somebody with a young dog—ideally the same age as yours—have them over as often as possible.

After two or three weeks (you are the best judge of when your puppy is ready for more action) you can extend your walks and go around a whole block. **Do not** take your puppy along to the supermarket. You'd have to tie it up outside, and the danger of someone stealing

it is too great. Besides, the puppy is too young to be left alone in a completely unfamiliar place. If you absolutely have to get a few things to keep from starving to death, ask if you may take the puppy into the store, carrying it in your arms. (With a Newfoundland puppy this of course presents some difficulties, and you might want to leave it with a neighbor or a neighbor's child while you shop. Or your neighbor might wait with the dog in front of the store.) As long as the dog can't touch any food items, some store owners may allow a dog in their store.

Now you can take your puppy to parks and other places dogs visit. But don't take it on long hikes! One sometimes sees dog owners, especially those with large breeds, taking their puppies on marathon walks hoping to wear them out. But too much exercise does real harm to the bones and joints of young dogs. The bones are still soft and can easily become deformed if they have to carry weight too long. If you watch young dogs play you will notice that

Zwerg Spitz

they keep taking breaks in their play, lie down a bit, watch the other dogs, and then join in the game again. It's all short-term exercise. You wouldn't take your two-year-old on long hikes for the same reason. If the park is a long way from your house, drive there or take the bus or subway, but don't walk too far. When you get to the park, your main goal should be for your dog to play with the other dogs, not walk. (You have years and years ahead of you of walking with your dog. Be patient!) Wait until your dog is at least six months old before taking it on "real" walks. Before that, don't walk with it for more than half an hour at a time. That is quite enough. At this age a dog should play until it gets tired, not walk or run itself ragged.

It is better to play with your puppy than to take it on long walks.

Encounters with Other Dogs

When your puppy meets other dogs you have to restrain your impulses and stay out of the picture as much as possible. Young dogs usually approach other dogs with wagging tail, lie on their backs, let the other dogs sniff their bellies, and then, depending on their personality, may transform themselves into impudent roughnecks. Their teeth are needle-sharp—as you have no doubt discovered—and some dogs respond with a rebuke and growl to being pulled by the ears. Puppies tend to overreact, just to be

on the safe side, and start squealing pitiably before anything at all has happened. Most dogs are nice toward puppies, and those that prefer not to have anything to do with them usually go away. You should keep your puppy from getting cocky and following a disinterested member of the species, or it may find out the hard way someday that some older dogs are immune to its charms. But that is all part of growing up. A box on the ears now and then and some bouts of wrestling are all part and parcel of a healthy canine life and play an important role in teaching

Golden Retrievers

Boxers

your puppy limits, its own as well as those of other dogs. A dog that is picked up every time another dog the owner doesn't approve of approaches will become timid and tend to bite out of fear. Up high in your arms it will feel very powerful and yap down on the "enemy" who may not be an enemy at all. That dog may not take kindly to such treatment, and you may find yourself in the midst of a most ferocious dog fight before you know it. The more direct experiences a puppy has with other dogs, the better off it is later in life.

It's the same as with people.

Leaving the Puppy Alone

Leaving a puppy alone is not an easy matter. You have to learn how to do it, and it is possible to make big mistakes. Basically the same principles apply as with small children. If they (dogs or children) experience fear of being abandoned, this feeling seems to go deeper and is harder to overcome than if they are left alone at an age

when their trust and self-confidence have grown stronger. All the dogs I know that bark for hours on end when left alone, driving the neighbors crazy, or tear half the apartment to shreds are animals that were left alone when they were only ten, twelve, or sixteen weeks old.

I know I am treading on dangerous ground here, but it is my firm conviction that dogs should not be left alone before they are six months old. Under no circumstances should you sneak out after your puppy has gone to sleep. It would be seized by panic when it woke up with no one around. From then on it would stick to you like a burr, following your every step, afraid it might lose you again. A dog that always has a human around during these early crucial months will grow up trusting that its mistress will be there when really needed.

Going away is best practiced with another person who will stay with the dog while you go away for a while. Don't make a dramatic scene when leaving. Simply explain to the dog "I have to go now, but I'll be back

soon" and close the door behind you. The person staying with the dog should not pay special attention to it but just play with it a little if it cries because you have left.

If you have converted a playpen into a dog kennel, you should put your puppy in it now and then and for the next few hours go in and out of the room where it is confined. If it pays no attention to your comings and goings, all the better. If it looks after you with pricked ears, tell it always in the same words ("I'm leaving but I'll be right back") that you have to be gone for a little while. The puppy can still hear you in the apartment and will therefore not be upset. The point of the exercise is for it to learn that it can't be with you all the time. It will understand very quickly that the phrase "I'm leaving but I'll be right back" means nothing earthshaking but simply that you'll be gone for a while but will be back. When you come back, don't make a big deal of that either; just say "Hello" to the dog and then go about your business (you weren't gone for three weeks, after all). Leaving the room is normal, and so is coming back.

Playing

Playing is just as important for your puppy—and later for the grown dog—as it is for children and grown-up people. It is through play that young animals acquire

Old English Sheepdogs

the skills and rules required to play the different roles of adult life. As a child you probably played at being a pirate, nurse, circus director, mother, father, and child. Instead of these make-believe games, puppies play chasing and catching, tug-of-war, and pretend fighting. When your puppy was very young it learned all kinds of things in the course of playing with its siblings and mother; it learned how to sneak up and pounce on prey—even if the prey was its sister's tail end. It learned how to assume the submission pose in play fighting; it learned to use its new voice, to run and to stop motionless, to dig, to use its nose, and to realize when it is better to stop pulling one's mother's ears.

Quite apart from the fact that playing with one's dog is fun, there are other beneficial aspects. You learn to understand your dog better. Through play you can teach your dog how to deal with new situations, how to make decisions, how to become fearless, in other words, how to use its little brain. And in the course of it all you can establish yourself

as the alpha dog, the dominant figure.

Remember? Play prepares for real life (especially for a pirate's life). That is why play has to follow certain rules that you have to establish and then adhere to. **Don't let your puppy play with your hands or bite them.** Make sure the puppy doesn't do this with other people or your children either, who might let it. If you should get bitten in the heat of play, instantly make a great to-do about it, stop the game, cry and moan, and hold your hand. Puppies act just the same way if another dog hurts them the least little bit (or looks as though it might) or if the game gets too rough. Your puppy has to learn that your skin is much thinner than that of its siblings and other dogs. I'd also suggest that you not let the puppy grab hold of your arm in the course of roughhousing. This might be cute while the animal is still small and uncoordinated, but how are you going to explain to a full-grown Airedale Terrier that this trick is no longer cute and is in fact dangerous?

Only toys and things you clearly assign to that category are to be played with. Socks, towels, stuffed animals that belong to someone else are off limits. Everyone has his or her own possessions, and your dog has to learn to respect that. The best way to teach this is to say "No" firmly and take away the things the puppy may not play with, replacing them with something that it may have. Make it very clear what are play things and what are not. An older dog can tell which socks can be played with and which are your favorite hiking socks, but a puppy can't. Pet stores sell a great variety of toys. Most dogs love balls. Make sure the balls you get are the right hardness for the age and physical strength of your dog. There are some made of hard rubber that trigger panic in dogs smaller than spaniel size because they are so hard and heavy. Also, when you buy toys check if they can be bitten to pieces and if so whether the parts are digestible. (Veterinarians have some horror stories to tell about parts of toys stuck in the intestines of young

dogs.) You can buy squeaky rubber toys that last a long time and whose squeak box can be excavated only with the greatest patience and effort. There are also handsome pieces of rope with fat knots at each end that the dog can get a hold on while you pull the other end (whenever you play tug-of-war, you win because you are the leader of the pack) or that the dog can shake furiously as if it were shaking a prey animal to death. Most dogs also like soft toys. There are items made of artificial sheep fleece that vaguely resemble stuffed animals that all dogs seem to like. Other toys are velvety to the touch and come either in the form of balls or in abstract shapes that lend themselves beautifully to being carried around and chewed on.

Puppies are still too young for playing Frisbee; their eyes are not yet capable of following very fast movements. But any puppy will run after a toy you toss for it, and all puppies like to play tug-of-war. Empty toilet paper rolls make wonderful toys because they are hard to

get hold of and carry at first but can ultimately be conquered. You can smear a tiny bit of peanut butter (unsweetened!) inside, which will make the toilet paper roll even more attractive, and if the puppy finally

tears it apart, the paper is relatively harmless for the digestion.

And remember, this is not a democracy. **Play continues only as long as you say, and toys are removed between play sessions.** This is exactly

Gordon Setter

the way things function in a pack of dogs. When an old male dog (females usually don't play with puppies that are not their own) gets tired of playing, he gets up and leaves. Without discussion. Any attempt to change his mind is fruitless; on the contrary, it most likely earns one a swat on the nose.

The more you play with your puppy and the more different experiences it has, the more its intelligence is stimulated, the more attached it will get to you, the better you will learn to understand it, and the more closely its attention will be fixed on you. Find some downed tree or tree limb—anything to serve as a balancing beam— and let your dog practice **balancing** on it. Show it how by walking across, and it will follow. That will improve its sense of balance, and yours perhaps as well.

If you throw anything you want your dog to retrieve, always say "Fetch!" and be lavish with praise if the dog brings it back to you.

Blow up a **balloon** and let your puppy play with it. The puppy will be both puzzled and intrigued by the strange, slow movements of this "ball" and then scared out of its wits the first time a balloon pops. But after a few times the pop won't come as a shock anymore; in fact most dogs even try after a while to pop the balloon themselves.

To **play hide and seek**, another person has to distract the dog while you hide behind the sofa, a tree, or a hedge. Then call your dog—not too many times, so that it will listen for your voice and concentrate on listening. When it has found you, praise it to the skies, as if it deserved the Nobel Prize.

To teach your dog to **search for things**, begin by using dog biscuits or tiny pieces of hot dog. Place little pieces of dog biscuit or hot dog (the latter have a stronger smell and are therefore easier to find) in a relatively obvious spot and command *Search!* Once the

Children and puppies seem to be made for each other.

puppy has grasped what is involved, you can make the hiding places harder and harder to find.

When the puppy is somewhat older (five to six months) and better coordinated, you can teach it to **Catch!** Have it sit, and say "*Catch!*" as you toss tiny bits of dog biscuit toward its muzzle. If it doesn't know already how to catch, the first ten pieces or so will probably bounce off its face. But don't worry, it will soon get the hang of it. After a day or two it will start opening its mouth and try to catch the goodies. Once your dog has caught on, it will enjoy the game, and not just for the taste of the biscuits. Now you can toss a tennis ball when you say "*Catch!*" If the dog misses, try again. But when it catches the ball, jump up and down with

excitement, clap your hands, and congratulate it. Tell it it is the brightest dog that was ever born.

Now your expectations can move a notch higher. This time, when it catches the ball, tell it to come. Say "*Hold on*" when it comes toward you and then, "*Let go!*" when it is next to you, so that it will let the ball drop in your hand. If your playful teenager prefers to run away with the ball, put a leash on it. Then when you call and the pup tries to wander off sideways, you can pull it toward you gently. Just don't get annoyed and angry. Although you are both learning from each other, it is still all a game. So keep everything happy and light.

At this same age you can also start testing your puppy's **tracking ability**. Tie a hot dog to a string and pull

it behind you through the yard (or through the park, but there you run the danger of soon being followed by all the dogs in the vicinity). Make sure your dog can't see you doing this. Then show your dog the point where you started. (Try to remember your starting point correctly.) If the dog shows no interest at all it is either still too young or you have shown it the wrong place. (This game does not work with Pugs, English Bulldogs, and Pekingese, breeds that are no good for scenting because of the anatomy of their noses.)

If the puppy shows a desire to sleep, let it sleep. Don't force it to go on playing. As you know, it is still a baby, and babies need to sleep.

Feeding Your Puppy

Puppies have to eat a lot in order to grow big and strong. Everybody knows by now that dogs can't live on the leftovers of our food, but not everybody may be aware that table scraps are actually bad for dogs. The diet of your dog has to be as carefully thought about as that of your children. Dogs are not pure carnivores. They eat and digest practically everything, from meat to fish to grain, fruit, and vegetables. Just like people, dogs need different diets at different phases of their lives. A young, growing dog requires sufficient vitamins, minerals, and protein; as an adult, it needs less of these nutrients, and from about the eighth year on, its nutritional needs change again.

Water

The most important thing your dog needs is water. Without water the cells can't function. Sixty percent of an adult dog's body consists of water. If it loses 15 percent of this water, it will die. By contrast, it can lose all its reserves of fat or glycogen, half of its protein reserves, or 40 percent of its body weight and still survive. So make sure that fresh water is always available to your dog, and change the water daily.

Commercial Dog Food

Commercial dog food is available in bewildering forms and varieties. It can be classed in two basic categories, dry and canned. The composition of both is usually very similar, except for the moisture content. The moisture of canned food consists not just of water but also includes meat juices and broth, things that literally make a dog's mouth water. Dry food is more easily digested and reduces the amount of feces produced. But of course it tastes the same every day. It is very handy for treats because it comes in bite sizes and fits neatly into your pocket.

Commercial dog food is designed to meet the nutritional needs of the different stages in a dog's life. Thus you can buy "puppy" food, "junior" food for young adults, "adult" food for fully grown dogs, and "senior" food for dogs from about eight years on. The choice from among different dry foods, food flakes, and canned foods—not to mention treats, chewing items, and mineral and vitamin supplements—is truly overwhelming and rather confusing. Avoid the cheapest brands as well as no-name brands. These may list the same amounts of

protein, for example, as more expensive brands, but the proteins in them may be of a lower quality that your puppy can't fully utilize. Often, too, meat from cheaper sources is used. Generally you can tell the lower quality as soon as you open a can. To your eye the food inside may look appetizing enough (your dog, however, doesn't care whether the peas are green or yellow, the meat pink or brown), but the smell gives it away. Even if your dog should prefer a cheaper brand, stick with the better one. Pet foods are often made more palatable by the addition of spices, which are not especially healthy for dogs. Taste buds have nothing to do with nutritional needs.

Remember that children, too, would usually rather eat fast food and candy, but we all know enough not to just let them eat what they want.

Cooking for Your Dog

If you want to prepare your dog's meals yourself, you must realize that commercial

Salukis

foods are prepared by trained scientists in fully equipped research laboratories. Buy a canine nutrition book, a scale, measuring devices, and you're ready.

Protein is the most important item in a dog's diet. The food of a growing dog has to contain at least 30 percent protein, whereas a grown dog that is moderately active will get along with 15 to 20 percent protein.

You can give your dog a combination of fresh meat and food flakes designed for puppies. This way the dog will get the necessary nutrients, including **minerals**, without your having to consult tables on the nutritional content of different foods.

The following nutritional information represents only this author's opinion, so you should discuss with your veterinarian what amounts are appropriate for your dog. If you prepare your dog's meals yourself, you should know the importance and nutritional value of the various components. The following pages will help you with that.

Saint Bernards

Eggs

The yolk contains important enzymes and the white is high in protein, but egg white has to be cooked before it is fed to dogs because it contains substances that destroy the B vitamins and digestive enzymes.

Linseed

Linseed supplies not only roughage but also crucial amino acids that can be beneficial for the skin and coat of your puppy. In addition, the high fiber content stimulates digestion.

Wheat Bran

Wheat bran, which is also high in fiber, helps regulate digestion as well and supplies phosphorus.

Oatmeal

Like pasta and rice, oats are an important source of carbohydrates. Because of their high fiber content they provide good roughage, but they are low in vitamins and minerals.

Cottage Cheese (low-fat)

This cheese is high in protein and low in lactose. Too much lactose often causes diarrhea in dogs. But low-fat cottage cheese is an ideal food for dogs with digestive problems.

Green Vegetables

Peas, spinach, zucchini, and other green vegetables are very high in minerals and vitamins.

Carrots

These provide good roughage (which aids the digestion) and are high in beta carotene. But the vitamins in carrots are fat-soluble, which means that they cannot be absorbed by the body unless there is fat in the diet.

Salad Oil

Oil supplies not only fats but also needed carbohydrates and important amino acids.

Poodle

Simple Recipes

60% beef stew meat
20% unrefined cooked rice
1 egg yolk or 1 hard boiled egg
5% linseed or wheat germ
1 tbsp sunflower, thistle, or corn oil
5% green vegetables (peas, spinach, zucchini, etc.)
Ask your veterinarian for a vitamin supplement to add

or:

50% beef heart/30% oatmeal
5% low-fat cottage cheese/5% linseed or wheat germ
3% carrots/1 tbsp salad oil
plus vitamins

or:

25% hamburger or beef neck/25% cooked rice or noodles
20% low-fat cottage cheese/30% grated apple
plus vitamins

Remember, these aren't scientifically formulated diets, so check with a veterinarian before feeding them. Vitamin and minerals supplements should also be prescribed to fit the diet.

When the puppy is six months old, you can start giving it various organ meats like heart, liver, kidneys, and meat from the head in moderate amounts, as well as lung or omasum (the third section of the stomach of cud-chewing animals). The latter is not very appealing to humans but smells yummy to dogs. Meat and chicken should be cooked briefly or braised. This makes them easier to digest. At first, cook carrots as well, and give them raw only gradually because they can wreak havoc with the digestive system of a puppy that is not used to them. Pork must never be given raw because of the danger of transmitting pseudorabies. Because poultry may be infected with salmonella, it is important to cook it as well.

Rice

Rice contains carbohydrates and is therefore a source of energy. In brown, or natural, rice the hull and the germ have not been removed, and therefore many important vitamins and minerals are preserved.

Pasta

Pasta is made up mostly of carbohydrates and is therefore an important supplier of energy.

Apples

These contain many fibrous substances as well as vitamin C. Grated apples given raw also regulate intestinal activity (a wonderful remedy for diarrhea!).

Vitamin and Mineral Supplements

High-quality commercial dog food contains adequate amounts of vitamins, trace elements, and minerals, and there is no need to add supplements to the food. An excess of these supplements can in fact be harmful, particularly for growing dogs. Some well-meaning dog owners mix mineral or calcium preparations by the spoonful into their dogs' food. Before adding any supplements, talk it over with your veterinarian. The secret of promoting good bone growth in young animals is to supply calcium and phosphorus in the right proportions. The body also needs vitamin D to absorb

Great Pyrenees

Bolognese

calcium properly, but too much of this vitamin can be harmful.

Human Food for Dogs

The basic rule is that you may give your dog anything to eat that you would feed to your small child—except, of course, sweets. These are an absolute no-no not only because they lead to obesity and ruin the teeth (and your dog would have great difficulty explaining to you that it has a toothache) but also because some sweet foods can actually be poisonous for dogs. That is the case, for instance, with chocolate. Strong spices and heavily salted foods are also bad for dogs. Milk causes

Irish Setters

diarrhea in most dogs because of the high lactose content.

bananas (lots of carbohydrates but also high in calcium), crusts of whole-grain bread plain or with a tiny bit of

liverwurst smeared on them, raw carrots, pieces of apple, and rawhide bones.

Snacks

If you feel you have to give your dog snacks now and then, use dog biscuits, but subtract the amount of calories they contain from the regular meals, or your dog will follow the pattern of people who tend to gain weight: They don't overeat at meals but do reach into the cookie jar in-between and then wonder why their girth is increasing. Other foods that can be given as snacks are raw knuckle bones (see facing page), dried tripe,

Beagles

Bones for the Dog

People automatically associate dogs with bones, yet dogs should be given bones only with precautions. It's true that gnawing on bones provides excellent massage for the gums, and all dog owners know that bones that have lain buried somewhere in the garden for several months taste as good to a dog as does a well aged bottle of red wine to many a dog owner. But just as red wine is not always the best thing for humans, bones can have dangers for dogs. Bits of bone that have splintered off can cause diarrhea or, in a worst-case scenario, cause punctures in the stomach or intestines.

Pekingese

◆ Pork or poultry bones must never be given to dogs. Cooked bones are off limits because they crush easily and the shards are dangerous to gums and other soft tissue, and poultry bones are bad because they splinter easily and can get stuck in the esophagus or the windpipe.

◆ It is best to buy only raw knuckle joint beef bones. These are soft and don't splinter. The marrow is also a good source of magnesium.

◆ Don't give your dog bones more often than once a week (danger of constipation!).

◆ When giving bones, always check the dog's feces; if they are too hard, stop feeding bones.

Your Puppy's Health

After your puppy has been with you a few days and has gotten used to its new life, you should take it to a veterinarian. Take along a stool sample in a small, clean jar with a lid and the puppy's immunization papers you received from the breeder. The veterinarian will examine the feces for parasites and may prescribe worming. He or she will also check the lymph glands, listen to the puppy's heart, and do a general check-up that includes weighing the puppy and taking its temperature. Teeth and gums will also be examined and the coat checked for signs of fleas. The veterinarian will then discuss with you what needs to be done.

A veterinarian is no miracle doctor, but he or she does know a great deal. Ask when it is time for the next set of immunizations. If you are considering neutering the animal, discuss that.

Check whether you are giving the right amount of food for this particular dog, and ask about flea medications that are safe for puppies. Your veterinarian will play a fairly important role in your life, so you should make this first visit as pleasant as possible for your puppy. If the waiting room is empty, let the puppy wander around and sniff everything. If there are other dogs or other animals, it is better to hold onto your puppy. Many animals associate the veterinarian's office with bad experiences (shots, painful treatment of wounds, etc.) and are therefore tense and not in a mood to put up with the antics of a silly little puppy. So keep your puppy close to you and keep it occupied with a toy you've brought along, a scrap of paper, or a chew stick.

The health of your dog is your responsibility. It is up to you to keep its coat shiny, its eyes bright, its ears clean, and you have to watch out to make sure that it doesn't eat anything poisonous, that it is wormed every six months or so, and that its immunizations are up to date. Much depends on proper diet but also on how you treat your young dog.

Treat your puppy very gently physically. Don't do anything with it you wouldn't do with a small child. **Don't ever** pick it up by its front paws; you might dislocate its joints. Don't let it jump off furniture because it could sprain its front paws. As I said earlier, don't take it on long hikes because its bones and joints are not yet up to that much exercise. Playing is much less stressful for the bones than walking and running. If you watch your dog when it's playing, you will be struck by how often play is interrupted with rest breaks, how often your puppy will lie down for a while and let its playmates

run by without joining in the action.

Climbing stairs is also off limits. A dog's skeleton is not designed for climbing stairs. Until the bones are really solid and strong, climbing stairs can aggravate hip and back problems, especially hip dysplasia. The heavier and more long-boned the breed, the greater the weight the immature bones have to carry. After about six months the bones firm up sufficiently, and then stair climbing is permissible. But until then you'll have to carry your puppy up and down stairs. (I hope you don't live on the fifth floor of an old apartment building without an elevator and that the dog you have acquired is not a Saint Bernard. If you should find yourself in this situation, you will save yourself the cost of joining a fitness center but will probably need the services of a chiropractor.)

Taking a puppy along when bicycle or horseback riding is also out of the question. You wouldn't take a young child along jogging, would you? As long as internal organs like the heart and lungs are not yet fully developed, a young dog should run only as much as it feels like and no more. When it gets tired, don't urge it to keep going. At the age of about twelve months your dog is no longer a young child, and then you can start realizing your athletic ambitions, as long as you start gradually. But before that time, let your dog set its own pace; after all, you don't want to risk its developing heart problems.

Beagles

Illnesses

Allergies

Dogs, like people, can develop all kinds of allergic reactions with various degrees of severity. Symptoms include minor or major subcutaneous welts, asthma, and skin reactions, such as intense itching or swollen areas around the eyes or muzzle. If there is swelling at the muzzle, quick help is needed because usually the respiratory passages swell up along with the muzzle. Allergies can be caused by countless things (allergens), such as pollen, fleas, dust, wool, and some foods. Some dogs are even allergic to cats. Allergies should be treated by the veterinarian.

Diarrhea

Diarrhea is usually the result of a dog having eaten something it shouldn't have. The best way to cure it is to give the dog a charcoal tablet. The charcoal binds some poisons in the body. Then give either nothing to eat for twenty-four hours or a mild diet of rice and chicken meat. If the diarrhea persists, call the veterinarian. Although diarrhea is usually nothing more than a sign of an upset stomach, it can be a symptom of a more serious problem. Make sure your dog does not get dehydrated. Diarrhea drains a lot of fluid from the body and is particularly dangerous in the case of young dogs. Pull the dog's skin up. If it snaps back elastically when you let go, your dog is all right; but if the skin feels stiff and returns to its normal position only slowly, your dog is dehydrated and you have to get it to the veterinarian immediately to have the fluid level restored intravenously.

Vomiting

Like diarrhea, vomiting is nothing serious in dogs and normally simply means that the dog has eaten something that didn't agree with it. Dogs routinely vomit after eating grass, which seems to be a regular ritual. Perhaps they eat grass to clean out

Maremma Sheepdogs

the stomach. Watch your dog. If it vomits more than two or three times, call the veterinarian because this may be a sign of a more serious disorder. If there is blood in the vomit, you have to take the dog to the veterinarian right away.

Infectious Diseases

The diseases against which you have to have your dog vaccinated are serious indeed. Fortunately, most of them hardly ever occur anymore in the Western world, now that most dogs are routinely vaccinated. However, with the many animals imported in recent years from elsewhere, there has been an increase in cases of distemper and canine hepatitis, probably because many puppies imported by animal dealers had forged health records, had contact with infected dogs, or had not been vaccinated at all.

In immunization or vaccination, viruses or bacteria that have been attenuated or killed are injected, and the dog's body responds by forming

antibodies. If a dog that has been vaccinated comes in contact with a disease carrier, the manufacture of antibodies is stimulated anew. If the immunity is

wearing off, however, the body can't produce antibodies fast enough, and the dog gets sick. That is why annual, or biannual, booster shots are necessary.

Pastore di Ciarplania

Distemper

Distemper is caused by a virus and is, in some countries, considered eradicated. Many veterinarians had until recent years never even seen a dog with distemper. Now, however, the disease is observed again with greater frequency, introduced probably through puppies that dealers bought without vaccinations in other countries and sold with falsified papers. Distemper is particularly pernicious for young dogs. The incubation period from contact with the virus carrier to outbreak of the disease is about two weeks. Distemper initially manifests itself in flu-like symptoms and a light fever that lets up soon, and the dog seems to regain its health. When the disease enters its next phase, the dog is obviously and seriously sick. It suffers from diarrhea, often bloody, and vomits. Then the eyes and nose emit a sticky pus-like discharge that often glues the eyes quite shut and obstructs breathing. The dog becomes apathetic and stops eating. Through a combination of diarrhea, vomiting, and refusal to eat the dog usually becomes severely dehydrated. These symptoms are accompanied by cramps and convulsive seizures. If your veterinarian succeeds in combating the disease, recovery usually takes many weeks. As time progresses, the dog seems to be feeling better, but this reprieve is usually followed by a relapse characterized by cramps and other nervous spasms that can result in death. A dog that has survived distemper is often left with nerve damage or teeth that show major loss of enamel, so-called "distemper teeth."

Hepatitis

Hepatitis is a contagious liver disease that is transmitted from dog to dog through urine, feces, or saliva. The disease runs a course similar to that of distemper. A recently infected dog develops red eyes, a discharge from nose and eyes, and a high fever. It grows apathetic, stops eating, and, in very severe cases, sinks into a coma. Within six to ten days the dog either dies or experiences eventual recovery. Opacity of the cornea often remains as permanent damage.

Leptospirosis

Unlike distemper and hepatitis, leptospirosis is caused by bacteria and is therefore easier to treat pharmaceutically. But it has become so rare that many veterinarians have never actually encountered a case in practice. The disease is spread through contact with an infected dog or with infected urine and often manifests itself first in apathy and refusal to eat. The muscles of the hind legs tend to develop weakness. This is generally followed by ulcers and sores in the mouth, stomach, and intestines, accompanied by bloody diarrhea and a foul, carrion-like smell from the mouth. The eyes turn yellowish. The damage caused to the gastrointestinal tract and the liver and kidneys hinders quick recovery, and even if a dog regains its health it can pass the disease on to other dogs through its urine.

Siberian Huskies

Rabies

Vaccination against rabies is required by law. Rabies is a viral disease transmitted in the saliva of an infected mammal such as a dog, fox, raccoon, or bat. Rabies is also contagious to humans, who after contact with an infected animal have to undergo a series of painful serum injections. There is no known method of treatment, and the disease is always fatal.

The first symptoms you are likely to observe are changes in the animal's behavior. A shy dog may become aggressive, or a lively extrovert may suddenly appear extremely shy and timid. The sick dog grows increasingly apathetic and unresponsive, can't bear being touched, develops diarrhea, and starts to vomit. Eventually it collapses, sinks into a coma, and dies. Rabies is a horrible disease, and any animal lover must do everything possible to protect his or her pets as well as other animals against it. Should you see an animal behaving oddly in the woods or anywhere else outside (any wild animal, such as a coyote, fox, raccoon or squirrel that doesn't run away when approached), call the warden in charge of the area or the police or town officials as soon as you can.

Parvovirus

This disease is sometimes called "feline distemper," but this is a misnomer. Parvovirus was unknown until 1978 but has now spread to all corners of the world. It is transmitted through contact with contaminated dog feces, which are easily carried indoors on the paws of dogs or the shoes of humans. Apparently even dogs that are not infected but that carry the virus can spread the disease to other dogs. A parvovirus infection starts somewhat like the flu, with a high fever, bloody diarrhea, and vomiting. Young dogs may die suddenly of heart failure, and the danger of death is high overall because of dehydration caused by the loss of fluid resulting from diarrhea and vomiting. Treatment is problematic,

---

If You Have to Call the Veterinarian

◆If an emergency situation arises, you have to call your veterinarian immediately. Stay as calm as you can, and give the veterinarian or assistant as much information as you can before setting out to the veterinary clinic. This way the veterinarian is able to make the necessary preparations.

◆The following should be considered emergency situations: acute stomach or abdominal pain, suspected poisoning, snake bite, burns, frostbite, shock, dehydration, repeated vomiting, continued bleeding, and deep wounds.

◆You are the best judge of your dog's state of health, so don't hesitate to call your veterinarian if anything looks suspicious to you.

but fluid therapy helps. Some dogs come down with a relatively mild case of the disease and recover well. Others sustain chronic intestinal damage, and some die.

Bordatella

Bordatella, or kennel cough, is transmitted from dog to dog and is usually no worse than the flu in humans. But kennel cough is highly contagious and spreads very quickly. Signs include a hard, dry, hacking cough, sometimes accompanied by a discharge from the nose. Adult dogs recover relatively quickly, but puppies should be kept in a warm, not too dry environment (use a humidifier!). Kennel cough is caused by a combination of various viruses and bacteria and is treated with antibiotics prescribed by the veterinarian. You should have your dog vaccinated against bordatella if you plan to take it to a kennel, but of course it may get infected anyway. The bordatella virus, like the flu virus, changes constantly, and finding an effective vaccine can be difficult.

Immunizations

The purpose of immunization is to protect your puppy or adult dog against more or less life-threatening infectious diseases.

When you get your puppy, it should already have had its first vaccination. Further immunization should follow according to schedule, and between four and six months of age, rabies vaccination is given. As a rule your dog will be given a kind of immunization cocktail that consists of five different vaccines listed for

A Typical Dog Immunization Schedule

Vaccination	8th week	12th week	16th week	annually	every two years
Parvovirus	●	●	●	●	
Distemper	●	●	●		●
Hepatitis	●	●	●	●	
Leptospirosis	●	●	●	●	
Bordatella	●	●	●	●	
Rabies			●	●	

brevity's sake as P, D, H, L, and R in the vaccination record. If you want to add a vaccination against kennel cough, you should mention this to your veterinarian.

Teething

At about three months your puppy will begin teething. Don't worry if you find one of its teeth now and then; actually most of them are simply swallowed by the animal. In children the first teeth to go are usually the front teeth; similarly in dogs, the incisors are first to go. In any case, a dangerous time begins now for your chair and table legs. Teeth growing in make the gums feel incredibly itchy, which is why puppies this age will gnaw on anything that they can find. To try to minimize damage to your furniture, give your dog a good supply of rawhide bones so that it will not be tempted to chew on the legs of your pretty, treasured Empire-style chair. Veterinarians sell dental-care strips made of various kinds of grain and containing enzymes. Most dogs accept

these strips happily, even dogs that generally disdain rawhide bones. Raw knuckle bones are also wonderful. Puppies can't chew them to pieces no matter how hard they work on them, and the

Saint Bernards

smell and taste must be simply heavenly (at least that is the impression one gets watching a dog gnaw on them for hours at a time). Steak bones on the other hand are inappropriate because they often have sharp edges, and poultry bones are not acceptable because they break into

splinters and can cause choking to death. Pork bones are off limits too because dogs must not be given raw pork. (For more on bones, see the chapter on diet.)

Parasites

Parasites are organisms that live on or in the dog and keep recurring in the course of the animal's life. They are relatively harmless as long as a dog gets rid of them promptly.

Fleas

We all know that dogs get fleas. Some people say dog fleas are not interested in humans, just as cat fleas supposedly leave humans and dogs alone. I personally consider this wishful thinking. If a flea has nothing better around, it cares little about the source of its meal, as you can readily observe from the small, round bite marks, usually in sets of three, that appear on your ankles and itch ferociously. Fleas can live two years, though they can lay eggs only if they find the right blood to feed on. That is why the breeding grounds of fleas are usually where your dog spends most of its time. Fleas are bad not only because their bites cause skin reactions like itching and allergies but also because they act as vectors for tapeworms.

Fleas are normally big enough to be visible to the naked eye as small black dots that move by crawling or hopping. In most cases, though, you will first spot their excreta. If you find tiny, black bits of matter in your dog's coat, you can be fairly

Salukis

sure that your dog has fleas. Summer is when fleas are most active, from June to September. Ask your veterinarian to recommend a flea control program. I would urge you not to buy flea remedies from regular stores. Fleas are resilient beasts, and the substances used to combat them are potent and sometimes poisonous, especially for children, and therefore potentially so for your dog. Puppies, especially, should be treated only with medications from your veterinarian. If your dog already has fleas, first give it a bath with a flea shampoo and then douse it with a flea spray. And be sure to wash the dog's pillows and blankets to get rid of the flea eggs. One female flea can lay 400,000 eggs a day, and you surely don't want them in your home.

Ticks

Ticks are another plague dogs suffer under in many places. Ticks can live as long as two hundred days without eating. Usually they live in tall grass and in bushes and drop onto the dog when they sense it approaching. Small pincerlike organs help them burrow the head underneath the dog's skin, where they suck blood. After sucking themselves full they are no longer brown but gray, the size of a pea, and disgusting looking. When full of blood, they drop off the dog and lay between one thousand and three thousand eggs.

Tick bites can get badly infected, and ticks also transmit borreliosis and Lyme disease to dogs. They have to be removed promptly, but this is not easy because they burrow into the skin with their head. The best way is to use tick tweezers, available at pet shops. Get a hold of the tick's body with the tweezers and then rotate the tweezers several times. Once the tick is thus "unscrewed" it is best flushed down the toilet. Ticks are found most often on the head and around the neck of a dog. Veterinarians can prescribe a tick repellent that will protect your dog for an extended period of time with a single application. You should check your dog for ticks regularly during the warm months.

Flea Control

The fleas you find on your dog are only part of the problem, the smallest part!

◆ Wash and vacuum your dog's pillows and blankets regularly.
◆ Apply flea spray to the places of the rug where your dog sleeps a lot.
◆ Comb your dog with a flea comb regularly starting in the spring, so that you will notice flea droppings right away.
◆ Use flea control medication in accordance with your veterinarian's directions.

Mites

Mites are parasites that live in or on the skin. The most unpleasant is the Demodex mite, which reproduces in the hair follicles. These mites are found even in healthy dogs, but serious symptoms develop only in dogs whose resistance is lowered as a result of things like worm infestation or inadequate nutrition. First there is hair loss on the head, around the eyes, and on the hind legs.

The skin begins to get red, thickens, and becomes infected with pus. The condition can spread over the entire skin. Treatment is difficult and expensive, and relapses are common. However, these mites pose no danger to humans.

Other common mange mites are *Cheyletiella*, *Psoroptes*, and *Sarcoptes*. In order to differentiate these, scrapings must be taken from skin lesions and the mite identified under a microscope.

Treatments vary according to the species of mite and location of the lesion. Some require long-term therapy, which may include injections or oral medication, others can be managed with dips, baths, or other topical medications. Don't rely on patent medication!

Worms

Adult dogs have worms only occasionally and are not greatly bothered by them.

Alaskan Malamutes

But in puppies and young dogs a heavy worm infestation can interfere with the digestive process and with proper development. This is why young dogs should be checked for worms every three months.

Roundworms are very common, especially in puppies, because puppies may be infested through the dam's milk, or, more commonly, while still in the womb. The worms are only seen in the feces or in food that is vomited. They look like pieces of spaghetti 4–6 inches (10–15 cm) long with pointed ends. In rare instances, humans, especially children, can be infested with dog roundworms by consuming the parasite's eggs that are passed in the dog's stool. When infestation occurs, roundworm larvae can cause eye damage and skin lesions. Children should always wash their hands after cleaning up dog feces in the yard.

Tapeworms are transmitted by secondary hosts, such as fleas and animal carcasses. Fleas are the most common means of tapeworm transmission—if your dog has one parasite, he probably has the other. You can see sections of tapeworms in the dog's stool, where they look like white grains of rice about 5–10 mm long.

Other intestinal parasites found in dogs are **hookworms** and **whipworms**. These cause digestive problems and lead to emaciation. Your veterinarian can prescribe safe medications against worms. The hope that carrots or garlic would be effective against worm infestations has unfortunately proven illusory, although both are very good for your dog's health.

Emergency First Aid

Heavy Bleeding from Wounds

Exert pressure on the wound with your hand or a towel. When the bleeding has stopped, clean around the wound with a clean, damp cloth and apply triple antibiotic cream to the area. If the wound is deep, take the dog to the veterinarian, who can sew up the wound or clamp it shut.

First-aid Kit for Dogs

For emergency cases you should have the following available at home:
- charcoal tablets
- eye ointment
- gauze bandages
- Band-aids
- pads of absorbent cotton
- syringe (without the needle)
- fever thermometer
- scissors
- disposable plastic gloves
- tweezers
- towel
- tamed iodine ointment
- diarrhea medication

Suffocation

Most dogs, especially those with very short noses, will at some point in their life get something stuck in their muzzle or throat, anything from a chunk of food to a stick to a piece of a toy that was bitten off. The symptoms are unmistakable. The animal is unhappy and restless, usually rubs at its face with its paw, gasps for air, chokes or coughs, and looks at the world with

glassy eyes. Open the dog's mouth wide, reach as far into the throat with your fingers as you can, and try to remove the object that is stuck there. If you can't get hold of it or find nothing there, drive your dog to the veterinarian as quickly as you can.

Heatstroke

If a dog is left in a hot car or if it is urged to play too vigorously in very hot weather, it may suffer heatstroke. The signs of heatstroke are frantic panting, vomiting, and circulatory collapse. You have to lower the dog's temperature immediately, but not too drastically. Wrap it in cold towels or lay it in the bathtub and spray it with cold water, but not ice. Meanwhile call your veterinarian, who will give you further instructions. Probably he will prescribe medication to stabilize the circulatory system.

Never leave your dog in the car during hot weather, even if the windows are left open. Short-nosed breeds like Boxers, Bulldogs, and Pugs should be allowed to rest during the day when it's hot. Take them for walks in the morning and evening, when it is cooler.

Poisoning

Most puppies take everything they come across into their mouths. That is why you have to remove all poisonous substances from their environment. There are quite a few perfectly normal household items that are poisonous to animals. Surprisingly, even chocolate is dangerous. It is not only bad for a dog's teeth but is

Weimaraners

actually toxic. Dogs love chocolate, just as people do. But their digestive system is very different from ours. So keep chocolate out of your dog's reach, along with cleaning agents and poisonous plants. Poisoning manifests itself in vomiting, dazed behavior, sudden

Plants Poisonous to Pets

The following indoor and outdoor plants can cause poisoning in dogs:
- amaryllis
- boxwood
- Christ's-thorn
- ivy
- monkshood
- foxglove
- lilac
- laburnum
- honeysuckle
- hyacinth
- privet
- lily of the valley
- narcissus
- oleander
- philodendron
- spindle tree
- daphne
- spurge

cramps, or bleeding from various orifices. If you suspect poisoning, call the veterinarian immediately, so that she can get everything ready by the time you get there.

Insect Bites

Dogs often react violently to bee and wasp bites. The head swells up, and along with it the breathing passages. Such bites have to be treated immediately with an injection or with an antihistamine. Drive your dog to the veterinarian as quickly as you can.

Neutering

The subject of neutering or sterilizing is still one that people shy away from even in our modern, enlightened time. Neutering is always preferable to sterilization. In females, **sterilization** means the cutting of the ovarian tubes; in males, the cutting of the sperm duct. After this operation, female dogs still go into heat, and males still pursue them. **Neutering** means that a female's uterus

and ovaries are taken out or that a male's testicles are removed. These operations put an end to all sexual urges and activity. Contrary to a common belief, there is no health reason why female dogs "should be allowed to have puppies at least once." Worldwide, unwanted dogs have reached enormous numbers. These "excess" dogs are humanely destroyed by the millions each year. Only by controlling our pets' reproduction can we put an end to this problem. Actually, most female dogs are much better off not having to undergo the major hormonal changes that go along with estrus twice a year. Also, the incidence of mammary tumors is about 85 percent less in females that have been spayed. People often argue that neutering is not normal and is contrary to nature; but, for a female, going into heat twice a year without becoming pregnant is not exactly normal either; nor is it normal for a male to be aroused by the female's enticing smells and by the massive release of hormones triggered by them and never

be permitted to engage in any sexual activity.

In the case of males, the discussion usually becomes emotionally charged, especially when male dog owners are speaking. What they may find reasonable when it applies to female dogs is, to their minds, simply unacceptable where male dogs are concerned. But neutering, or castration, in no way affects a dog's personality. Immediately after the surgery dogs generally become quieter and often more interested in food, but that passes after hormonal production has adjusted. (It is not castration that makes a dog gain weight but getting too much to eat, which is under the owner's control.) Some male dogs that have not been neutered can become physically lovesick to the point of refusing to eat and turning apathetic and depressed.

Then too, life with a very aggressive and dominant male can become much easier if the dog is neutered because the sending of instinctual signals—such as a stiff-legged gait, raised hair on the back, tail standing up straight in the air—ceases along with the reaction to them. Dogs that are roamers no longer run away but instead concentrate their attention on their home and their people. You no longer have to get on your bicycle to go looking everywhere for Rover or appear at the local police station several times a week. Life suddenly becomes pleasant and relaxed, the neighbors say Hello again, and every day is a good day.

Giving Medications

Pills

The simplest way to give a dog a pill is to wrap the pill in a piece of cheese or some hamburger. Dogs swallow things whole and usually don't wonder what's inside a special treat. But you should still watch to make sure the pill has gone down. If your

---

Benefits of Neutering

The greatest benefit of neutering your dog is that the animal will definitely not have or sire any more puppies. There are too many puppies in this world already and too few good homes for them. Further benefits are:

◆ no trying heat periods for female dogs

◆ no admirers howling at your front door or following you for miles

◆ reduced risk of uterine and mammary tumors

◆ less territorial and aggressive behavior without change of personality in male dogs

◆ no more urge to take off on amorous pursuits

◆ reduced risk of urogenital diseases in male dogs

dog manages to separate the pill from the meat and keeps spitting it out, you'll have to open the dog's mouth wide, tilt its head backward, and put the pill as far back on the tongue as possible. Then shut the dog's mouth, hold the muzzle shut with some pressure, and massage the throat until you see the dog swallowing. Again check to see the pill is really gone.

Liquid Medication

The best way to give liquid medicine is with a syringe without the needle, which you can get from your veterinarian or from a drug store. Fill the syringe with the required amount of medicine, gently hold the dog's mouth shut, and stick the syringe (without the needle!) into the corner of the mouth between the teeth and the cheek. Then push the plunger. This way you keep the dog from choking or the liquid from going down the wrong tube.

Ointments

If you have to apply ointments to the eyes, gently pull the lower eyelid downward and outward, and squeeze the necessary amount into the little pocket formed by the eyelid. When the dog blinks, the ointment will automatically be spread over the eye. Applying ointments to the skin is simple. Just separate the fur in the places that need treatment, and rub the ointment into the skin as best you can. If the skin is raw or if there are open places, be especially gentle and careful.

Simple as it may be to apply ointment, the trick is to make sure the ointment stays there. A dog's first instinct is to lick it off instantly, thus further irritating the wound or sore and canceling the effect of the medication. To keep a dog from doing this, you can get a plastic collar from your veterinarian that looks a little like something from Queen Elizabeth's time. These collars prevent dogs from reaching most parts of the body and therefore from licking wounds or gnawing bandages off. Dogs, of course, hate the collars because they restrict their freedom of movement and make a big noise when bumped against chair legs and door posts. But they do help wounds heal faster.

You should go about these various operations with a smile on your face and as though they were the most natural thing in the world so that the dog doesn't get the impression that pills, ointments, and such are matters to worry about. Immediately after such a treatment do something else with the dog to get its mind off what just happened. Throw a ball for it or take it to the window and show it the traffic, anything you can think of.

Grooming

Having a dog also means taking care of its hygienic needs. Some people find this delightful and can hardly get enough of brushing and combing their Lhasa Apso, Bearded Collie, or Maltese. Other dogs are not thus spoiled and have to do practically all their grooming themselves.

Regular grooming has the advantage that you find

fleas, wounds, bruises, and so on right away. You can tell if your dog has an ear or eye infection and treat it before the dog's eyes begin to tear or the dog starts shaking its head because something in the ears doesn't feel right. Short-haired dogs generally need less coat care than long-haired ones. I say generally because the short-haired Shar Pei, for example, needs to be massaged regularly to get air between the folds of skin and prevent infection there. But even with normal short-haired dogs, some attention has to be paid to grooming.

Shar Pei

The **coat** generally mirrors the dog's state of health. The fur should be loose and glossy. **All** dogs shed except for Poodles, Havanese, and Chinese Hairless. You just notice it less with short-haired dogs. But there are exceptions here too. The hair of Dalmatians and Pugs, for example, is very short but also very hard and sticks to clothes so that it is practically impossible to get off. (For this reason, owners of Dalmatians would do well not to wear black, even though they would match the color scheme of their dog very well.) Most dogs shed in rhythm with the seasons, that is, they replace their coat in the spring and fall. Some breeds, though, those with a thick undercoat, lose some hair practically all year round. If your dog is shedding a great deal, this may be a sign that it is in poor health, was or is under stress (a dog show, a long car trip, a change in the weather, a fight with another dog), or lacks certain vitamins. A relatively inexpensive blood test can determine the cause.

So there is the problem of dog hair. But this can be dealt with easily by brushing the dog briefly every day. For very short-haired dogs (such as Boxers, Whippets,

A good brushing feels like a massage.

Pointers, and Dobermans) you need a soft rubber brush. On dogs with average short hair (such as Pugs, Terriers, Labrador Retrievers, Rottweilers, Corgis, and Akitas), use a brush with natural bristles, and on long-haired dogs (like Bearded Collies, Lhasa Apsos, Setters, Old English Sheepdogs, and Pekingese), a good-quality wire brush. Daily brushing removes the loose dead hairs and stimulates the hair follicles that release the oils that protect the dog from the cold and make its coat glossy. Get your dog used to the daily brushing ritual. At first the dog will probably not want to hold still and will be quite uncooperative. But daily repetition, a few firm words, and lots of praise will have the desired effect, and the dog will soon look forward to the brushing sessions. After all, brushing means a few minutes of your undivided attention and a pleasant massage.

Long-haired dogs need to have the hair around the anus trimmed short, matted hair thinned with a small, sharp trimming comb, and the hair on the ears combed out. Some breeds, like those of Tibetan origin, have to have the fur on their paws cut because the hair between the pads keeps growing. (These dogs were bred for the Tibet high country where they needed to keep their feet warm in sub-freezing temperatures.) This hair can get so matted that it forms clumps like small pebbles between the pads and is very painful.

In some breeds the hair has to be cut around the eyes with blunt-tipped baby scissors. You have to be very careful doing this. Often the ends of the cut hairs poke into the eye even more sharply and can lead to inflammation of the cornea. Whether Sheepdogs are in fact unable to see anything unless their hair is tied up is still a subject of debate. Lhasa Apsos have hair over their eyes as a kind of sun screen to protect the eyes against the glaring sunlight in the snowy heights of Tibet. These hairs are also quite useful because they filter out dust. In any case, I have run into a number of Sheepdogs and Lhasa Apsos with inflamed eyes because stubs of hairs kept poking into their eyes or because the hair tied up on their heads gave their sensitive eyes no protection against strong winds. By contrast I have rarely encountered members of these breeds that have run into trees because they were unable to see. (Let me mention just in passing that I wore a similar hairdo as a teenager and was able to see perfectly well. That my adolescent facial expressions were hidden from view was a welcome side benefit.)

Similar considerations apply to shearing long-haired dogs. Long fur functions somewhat like an air conditioner. The different layers of the coat simultaneously insulate and air the dog. Desert dwellers dress according to the same principle, always wearing several layers of thin wool clothing. The skin of long-haired dogs is often very sensitive to sunlight, and you should always keep this in mind during summer. One other reason against shearing is that the fur often grows back poorly after a number of trimmings. In

short, if you buy a Sheepdog you should reconcile yourself to the fact that this dog requires a lot of grooming and not try to turn it into a Schnauzer. The same applies to Bernese Mountain Dogs and Bouviers de Flandres. These dogs often prefer not to be too active in the summer because they are hot. Not overdoing exercise is also better for their heart.

When brushing, always keep an eye out for small wounds or sores (especially with long-haired dogs where such things are hidden by the fur), also for ticks, fleas, and flea droppings. Ticks are large enough to be noticeable, especially when they are full of blood. They spread diseases and cause inflammations and have to be removed promptly with tick tweezers. Fleas are harder to spot but usually leave behind secretions in the form of tiny black specks that give them away.

Ears

Examine the ears. Clean them at least once a week with a dry cotton ball and watch for dirt and inflamed areas. If you see a black, sticky substance with a strong smell, your dog probably has an ear infection that has to be treated by the veterinarian.

Eyes

Clean the eyes with some cotton and warm water. Check to see if the eyes are tearing, look irritated or red, or show a greenish discharge at the corners. These are a sign to take the dog to the veterinarian. Often, a corneal abrasion appears light blue. If you notice any change in eye color, take your dog to the veterinarian as quickly as you can.

Mouth

Look over your dog's teeth at least once a week. Pull the lips back to examine the gums. If there is some yellow plaque along the edges of the teeth or if the gums are pale or are bleeding, that is another reason for a visit to the veterinarian. All the problems mentioned here are quite rare, but you should check for them regularly.

Important: It is absolutely crucial that you train your dog to put up with the various examinations described here. If it refuses to cooperate, no veterinarian will be able to examine it without tranquilizing it. In an emergency this can be a matter of life and death. Do you want to watch your dog suffocate because it will unfortunately not let you pry open its mouth after a stick has gotten stuck sideways near the throat or has rammed itself into the roof of the mouth?

Bath Day

Although most dogs love taking mud baths, rolling in foul-smelling puddles, or going to the beach, many of them think there is nothing worse than a bath in the bathtub that involves soap or shampoo. But every dog needs a bath now and then because it has gotten into something disgustingly awful, has had diarrhea, raced around in so much filth that it is barely recognizable as a dog or because it was in heat, or

simply because it stinks. Old wisdom prescribed that you should give your dog one bath a year at most and that anything beyond that is unhealthy. But things have changed in our modern world. Shampoo for humans is in fact bad for a dog's skin and coat and should never be used. But in pet stores you can buy many different kinds of dog shampoo that are designed for the pH of a dog's skin and that can therefore be used without qualms. The streets of our modern cities are quite dirty, as any owner of a West Highland White Terrier, Maltese, or other short-legged, long-haired breed

will readily attest to. These dogs pick up dust, traces of gasoline and motor oil, splashes of puddles, and worse. The coat soon feels greasy and heavy, and the dog smells very doggy, as do the hands that have petted it.

But **puppies** are a somewhat different matter. They must not be bathed in wintertime, regardless of how dirty they may be. Puppies get cold very quickly, and that may increase susceptibility to respiratory ailments. The longer your puppy's fur, the longer it takes to dry. If your puppy is truly filthy, brush it very thoroughly; if it has rolled in something

indescribably horrible, try to clean the affected area with a wash cloth, warm water, and a little shampoo, but wait with a bath until the weather gets warmer.

It is usually easier to give a dog a shower bath either in the bathtub or a shower stall than to convince it to take a regular bath. Besides, you'll have to rinse the soap off anyway.

The first bath is usually a contest to see who has the stronger will, you or the dog. Place a rubber mat in the bathtub or in the shower stall, so the dog won't slip on the smooth enamel. Also have a big old towel ready and handy next to the bathtub or shower. Now spray the dog with lukewarm water (hand temperature) until it is wet down to the skin, and rub in the shampoo. Make sure no water or soap gets into the eyes or ears. If necessary, stuff some cotton into the ears, and tilt the head up and backward when you rinse the dog off, so nothing runs into the eyes.

Shampoo the neck and shoulders first, then massage along the legs and down the

Most dogs suffer through a bath with howling and teeth chattering.

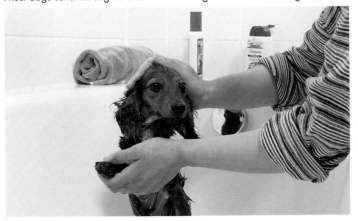

rest of the body all the way to the tail. Be sure also to get at the armpits, around the genitalia, and at the anal region and the base of the tail. Long-haired dogs should then be given a special conditioning rinse to keep the fur from matting. Finally, rinse with water until it runs clear and free of soap.

Drying

Before you lift your dog out of the bathtub, the animal should shake itself there, probably getting you soaked, but then who said that keeping a dog was always pure pleasure? Squeeze as much water out of the coat as you can without torment-ing the animal. Dry the dog off with a towel. This is probably the best part of the ordeal from the dog's point of view. Most dogs love to be rubbed with a towel, the more vigorously, the better. But be careful with dogs that have long hair. These dogs must only be patted dry because real rubbing gets the fur all matted and knotted.

If the weather is warm, you can now let your dog outside, where it will race around like crazy and thus get good and dry.

If it's cold outside, keep the dog inside, where it will also run around like a banshee, roll on rugs and carpets, rub against things, and generally behave as if it has just come home after a long exile. Don't let the dog out into the cold air for the next six to eight hours. In the winter it is best to bathe a dog in the evening to make sure it will be thoroughly dry by the next walk in the morning.

If you'd like to dry your dog with an electric hair dryer, you are welcome to do that. But most dogs are afraid of hair dryers. Turn the temperature to the coolest and the fan to the lowest setting and keep talking to the dog in soothing tones the whole time so it won't be too scared. Even though the bath will have gotten rid of many dead hairs, the dog should still be brushed thoroughly afterward. Bathing loosens a lot more hairs and makes dead ones fall out, and all of these can then be brushed out very easily.

Breton Pointers

The Anal Sacs

When discussing the physical care of dogs it is sometimes difficult to avoid indelicate subjects. But dogs do have anal sacs. They are located on both sides of the anal opening and produce a viscous secretion with an unpleasant smell, though dogs don't quite see it this way. To them it is a most delicious and important smell, a kind of identity card and the reason why dogs immediately sniff each other's tail end upon meeting. Sometimes the sac openings become plugged with fecal matter, resulting in overfilling. This feels very unpleasant and makes the dogs scoot, that is, slide the butt along the ground, or constantly lick the anal region. This behavior is usually a sign that the sacs have to be opened, a simple but not particularly attractive procedure. The veterinarian can do it for you, but if you want to save yourself the trip to his office and some money you can do it yourself.

First raise the dog's tail with one hand and have a towel or paper towel ready in the other. Then squeeze

Grooming Aids
- flea comb
- rubber curry comb
- brush (with wire or natural bristles)
- towel
- rubber mat
- scissors
- shampoo
- rinse
- absorbent cotton
- ear cleaner

gently on either side of the sac with your thumb and index finger (protected by a paper tissue), whereupon the secretion should appear. Afterwards you can carefully wipe the area clean. Plugged anal sacs can get infected and then have to be treated by the veterinarian. If the secretion is bloody or greenish, the squeezing is bound to be painful to the dog, and you should let the veterinarian deal with the situation. The entire procedure is simple but does require some practice. Have your veterinarian show you how so that you can do it yourself in the future.

If you follow all the suggestions and instructions given in this chapter with some regularity, you should have a healthy and stunningly groomed dog.

Training

Ah, obedience training! Nobody is very fond of this subject, which smacks of rigor and discipline, the carrot and the stick, hours of serious discussion with the dog—in short, which doesn't sound like fun at all. Most new dog owners think of obedience training as something akin to cruelty to animals and therefore don't train their puppy at all until it gets completely out of hand. That is nonsense, of course. Training has to be done with love, consistency, and firmness, never with cruelty or fits of temper, and never with the threat of dreadful punishment. Obedience training is more than teaching a dog to *Sit!*, *Stay!*, *Heel!*, and *Let go!* Obedience training is everything you do with your dog, everything the dog experiences, every game, every reprimand, every reward, every walk you take with it. Most of these things are fun, and as for the ones that are not so much fun, make them as enjoyable as possible. Every lesson you teach your puppy is the foundation stone for the next thing to be learned. The more playfully you approach training—the more you turn teaching into a game—the more you and your dog will enjoy the sessions.

Most dog owners realize that they are responsible for their dog's physical needs—food, water, medical care—but some still are not fully aware that they are also answerable for their pet's **mental** health and its behavior. The more different experiences your dog has and the more new things it encounters, the more relaxed and unflappable it will later be in unfamiliar situations. Have you ever noticed how calmly and stoically the dogs of homeless people behave when confronted with loud noise, police sirens, pedestrian crossings, and subways? Nothing shakes their equilibrium. These dogs have experienced just about everything: thunder and lightning without a roof over their heads (no music turned on so that the poor animal won't hear the thunder so loudly), nights spent in subway tunnels, insults from strange dogs, encounters with the police and with flying beer bottles, traffic jams, fog horns, and just about every other horror life in a big, modern city has to offer. Yet they generally look perfectly content and mentally stable. They are always with their master, who, after all, also sleeps while freight trains rattle past just a few feet away.

To put it bluntly, it's a crime not to train your dog. An ill-trained puppy grows into an ill-trained dog that constantly has to be kept locked away because it causes too much trouble otherwise, that can never be included in the family's activities, that runs out into

the road and gets hurt or possibly killed, or that eventually ends up in the animal shelter because it's simply too difficult to have around.

Puppies have to learn to take their place in the human pack. If you watch a group of dogs that live together, you will soon see how unsentimentally they deal with each other. Whoever doesn't toe the line, whoever goes against the group's rules, is quickly dealt with. Dogs are a lot less patient with each other than we are with them, and they don't argue.

A well-brought-up dog adds pleasure to your life. It can be taken along wherever you go; you can spend more time with it than if it lacked training, and you can keep teaching it new things that will make both of you feel proud (dogs are born show-offs). The better trained a dog is, the more reliable it will be and the more freedom it can be allowed. A well-trained dog can share more in your life and therefore leads a fuller life.

Training starts with **adjustment** and **socialization**. Many people don't know the difference between the two. A dog may have gotten used to children, to their playing, their noise level, and their activities (adjustment) and yet be much too wild and rambunctious when playing with them (lack of socialization). Adjustment to human activity and socialization early on are just as important as immunizations and a proper diet.

Adjustment

Getting your puppy used to something is quite simple. Just expose it to a situation and let nature take its course. As long as the experience is not painful or too scary, your puppy will later respond to this once new and unusual situation with indifference and learn to ignore it. If, for example, you live next door to your town's fire station, your puppy will soon get used to the sirens, the diesel fumes, and the large trucks roaring by the house.

Your dog has to learn to accept many new situations with the composure of a talk show host. Try to expose it to as many different situations as you can. Whenever possible, take it along with you to friends' houses,

Golden Retrievers

parking lots, and downtown streets, so that loud noises, confusion, and large crowds are no longer strange, let alone upsetting or fear inspiring. Life is a party, and parties are noisy. As long as your puppy is still very young, it's best to take along a basket, lined with a towel, into which you can set the puppy. This way it will be out of the way and won't get stepped on but can observe everything from a secure vantage point. Take it for walks on **streets with traffic** so that it can get used to the sound of cars. By the way, getting used to traffic is not the same as getting out of the way of cars. Your puppy would probably still run in front of a car if it were not on the leash.

Many dogs are afraid of **thunder**. You can keep this fear from developing by playing with the dog during thunderstorms to distract it and by not making a great fuss over thunder and lightning. If a thunderbolt is so loud that it shakes the house and it is impossible to act as though nothing had happened, say in a cheerful voice something like "Well,

what was that?" and go on playing.

In preparation for **leaving your dog alone** later on, it is a good idea now and then to leave the room where the puppy is and go about your ordinary business. You don't have to take the dog along to the bathroom. It knows you

Japanese Chin

are still there behind the closed door. When you feed the puppy, leave the kitchen and close the door behind you. The puppy will be distracted by eating and won't mind your absence so much. Give it a rawhide bone and leave it in the

room while you go somewhere else in the house, and so on.

Socialization

Like all of us, your dog needs certain social skills without which it simply

cannot live with people. A poorly socialized dog may start to bite either out of aggression or out of fear and will eventually no longer be able to live with your family. Your dog has to learn to tolerate and accept children even if you don't have any

yourself. Sometime in the course of life it will be confronted with children and the fact that children move quite unpredictably, that they are noisy, run fast, and may pull its ears or tail. Every dog **has to** accept that. A dog that bites children is always a hazard and rates as a failure in the pack. If you have children, your dog will get used to them all by itself. If you don't have any, ask your friends, neighbors, and relatives to come visit you with their children. Go to the zoo with the dog and the children, where your dog will be so overwhelmed by the amazing smells that it will be too busy to be afraid of the children or conclude that they are just silly. (A normal puppy doesn't find children silly since it is just like them.) If the neighbor-hood kids want to play with your puppy, encourage them to do so. But you should let them take your puppy for a walk only if they are at least twelve or thirteen years old and very responsible. Kids sometimes have strange notions. And so do puppies. Left to their own devices, the two can get into serious scrapes that may have dangerous consequences.

Some dogs get terribly excited when **company** comes. Let your dog be present when you have guests, but don't make a fuss over it. Let it know that this is your company, not its company, and that it will get its share of attention later. If the dog shows off, jumps up on the guests, or acts unruly, put it on the leash and have it lie down next to you without paying any further attention to it except for an occasional petting. Don't lock it away when guests come because that would teach it not to like company.

Other animals can become problematic for some dogs. If you and your dog are likely to encounter rabbits, chickens, goats, or horses on a regular basis, you have to get your puppy used to these creatures. Always do so casually, so the dog doesn't get the impression that there is anything special about the enterprise. Put the dog on the leash and keep walking past the animals until the dog gets bored and loses all interest in the leaping baby goats or clucking chickens.

Playing with other dogs is essential training for good socialization.

Do this routinely at least once a week.

I hope you take it for granted that your dog will play with other dogs. A dog that doesn't get enough contact with others of its kind is likely to bite other dogs, retreat into autism when in canine company, and thus be a potential problem whenever you take it for a walk. Ask your veterinarian if she knows anyone else with a puppy of approximately the same age as yours and if she could put you in contact with that person, so that the dogs can play together. Go for walks in parks, where there is always much dog activity, so that your puppy can learn the rules of canine social life, how best to behave with a stranger, and what it had better not do. All this is preparation for real life. It's not much fun trying to convince a full grown Leonberger that the subway is perfectly harmless or dragging him by the collar behind you because, being a country bumpkin, he is scared of city traffic. If your dog has been everywhere and done everything, it is not so likely to be frightened of things that make the hair on other dogs' backs stand up on end.

How Much Training Does a Dog Need?

When you first bring your puppy home, you have a choice. You can either start training it right away or you can wait. If you decide to put obedience training off for a while, your little pet will acquire quite a few habits that you won't find so charming later on, things like chewing the fringe of the carpet, upsetting the garbage can and sorting through its contents, knocking children over, or racing past you out the door. It takes much longer to

---

5 Basic Goals of Training

1 Come!: The dog is to come when called by name or when it hears the command; it should come up to the person calling, so that the leash can be put on easily.

2 Sit!: The dog should sit promptly when told to, and it should sit down automatically when the person next to it stops.

3 Down!: The dog is to lie down on command.

4 Stay!: When hearing this command, the dog is to stay where it is told to even when there are distractions and when the person who has issued the command leaves or is out of the dog's sight.

5 Heel!: The dog should walk calmly next to the person without pulling on the leash, dragging behind, or continually trying to get ahead of the person leading it.

break bad habits once acquired than to stop your dog from doing things you don't want it to do in the first place.

If, instead, you decide to start training your dog from the very beginning, this will also show the animal its place in the pack right off, and later difficulties (which **are bound** to arise) will be easier to deal with. The secret of training very young puppies is to teach them what kind of behavior will elicit praise and petting and what behavior does not. If your puppy realizes that it will be praised if it sits quietly, it will learn to sit quietly. If it realizes that you will bend down and pet it if it jumps up on you, it will jump up on you—or anyone else—even when you have on expensive nylon stockings or

Boxer, Bearded Collie, and Golden Retriever

a white dress. (Especially if you wear white. Nothing seems to attract dogs as much as white clothing. If there is a group of four strangers and one of them has on white pants, the dog is bound to jump up on that person, though I have to admit that this observation has not yet been confirmed by scientific study.) Kindness and rewards in the form of praise and food are the magic element if you are trying to teach your dog something. Punishment never accomplishes anything and neither does impatience or losing one's temper. If you feel rushed or edgy, wait and postpone the *sit!* lesson to another day. Impatience never achieves anything (and this is the most impatient person on this planet talking). It is always better to do something because one thinks it's really fun than because one is afraid of punishment. Your aim is not military drill but getting a domesticated, civilized dog, which is the kind of dog most of us would like to live with.

Consistency Above All Else

Training your dog starts with training yourself always to be consistent. Dogs don't speak English, no matter how often you have heard people say "He understands every word I say." Dogs communicate through body language and listen to the pitch and tone of the voice talking to them. This can go so far that your dog may ignore your mother-in-law's *sit!* because her voice and intonation simply are too different from the way you say *sit!* Dogs learn commands by connecting a certain tone of voice with the execution of the command, over and over again. So if you sometimes say *sit!* but really mean *lie down!* or *go away!* don't be surprised if your dog doesn't learn to sit, or anything else.

Dogs are creatures of habit and love a predictable routine. At the bottom of their souls they are bureaucrats. They want to be fed always at the same time, to come home always at the same time, and they want the same word to mean the same thing every time they

hear it. So when you say *sit!* do you mean "sit down now" **or** "sit if you feel like it"? If the word that expresses your command means something different every time, your dog will stop listening to you and figure that you are unreliable and incompetent. For every command you want to teach your dog, you have to decide on a specific, clear, and preferably short word—it can be anything at all, something in Chinese if you like—but you have to be able to remember it and use this same word every time.

If you want to have a dog that obeys consistently, you have to be consistent yourself and make sure a) that the dog understands what you mean and b) that every command is correctly executed. If you get your dog to come every time you call it and if you reward it every time, the dog will enjoy coming. If you allow it **not** to come right away when you call, it will for the rest of its life come only when it feels like it. This means that you'll have to go after it many times, put it on the leash, and drag it back to the spot where you called it, and

repeat over and over "Come, Rover, come."

You probably haven't been told before that you'll have to train yourself first in order to train your dog, have you?

Housebreaking the Puppy

During the first few days, a young puppy seems to have to urinate all the time. Hardly have you come in with it from outside when it starts looking around again, with rounded back and an air of great concentration, for a suitable place to make a puddle.

Housebreaking your puppy requires your full attention. But the work of three or four days will pay off for the rest of your dog's life. The principle is really quite simple. Immediately after an eight to ten-week-old puppy has eaten, drunk, woke up, or stopped playing, it has to go. There is no point in arguing, and you must **never** punish it for urinating. The time when people picked up their dog, rubbed its nose in the mess, and yelled at it are

gone for good. None of this does any good, and in terms of canine etiquette it is terrible manners to boot. Your puppy will long since have forgotten what it did that aroused your ire, and all you are teaching it is to be afraid of you, which is exactly what it is **not** supposed to learn. Until a puppy is about twelve to fourteen weeks old the muscles of its bladder are not strong enough yet to control the release of urine. That's all there is to it. If the puppy has an accident, it's **your** fault. It is your job to take the puppy outside in time.

So as soon as your puppy has eaten, drunk water, slept, or played, pick it up and take it outside, always to the same spot. Wait until it has relieved itself, and then praise it to the sky, as if it deserved a medal of honor. If you have a yard or garden, that makes things easier. Leave the door open, and if the puppy has always been taken to the same spot, it will soon go out by itself every time it feels the urge. (All this is a bit more difficult if there are steep

stairs leading outside. Most puppies are afraid of stairs, which they shouldn't climb anyway because their bones are not up to it yet.) Friends of mine who live on the fifth floor tried to house train their Bouvier des Flandres puppy. But by the time they got to the elevator with the dog (which was already quite large and heavy at ten weeks), reached the ground floor, and finally the street, the accident had usually already happened. In a case like this it is easier first to train the puppy to **use a box**, a method that works extremely well for very young puppies. Line an old box with low sides with several layers of newspaper, which you cover with dirt. Then put the box in a corner in the kitchen (as far away from the dog's bed as possible because dogs are very reluctant to relieve themselves near where they sleep—you would probably feel the same way). The dirt is very important so that the dog learns that this is the kind of stuff—soil, small stones, grass—it is supposed to look for when it has to go. Not rugs, not newspapers,

not tiles. As soon as you notice your puppy looking for a good place to make a puddle, pick it up and take it to the box. If it tries to climb out, put it back in with a firm "No!" After it has gone, praise it lavishly. Normally puppies understand the procedure after at most three days, and they march to their box all by themselves as soon as they feel their bladder getting too full.

If the puppy manages to get only one leg in the box and half of the mess ends up outside of it, you still have to praise it extravagantly for having tried. If you catch it about to go in another place, pick it up immediately with a clear "No!' and take it to its "bathroom," that is, the yard, street, or box. I have said before that dogs are creatures of habit. If your puppy has peed twice in the same wrong place without having been stopped, it will now consider this its bathroom. Clean the place thoroughly with glass cleaner or a disinfectant to get rid of every last trace of urine smell that might tempt your puppy to use that spot again. Any signs of recogni-tion have to be limited to the places where it is **allowed** to do its business. Even if you have set up a box, you still have to take your puppy outside regularly to urinate and defecate, and you have to do so in any weather, even when it rains, snows, and there is ice. And you have to stop and watch to make sure it has really done what you took it out for and also so that you can express your approval instantly and with appropriate enthusiasm. (You sure you wouldn't rather have a cat?) While you wait for your dog to get down to business, don't distract it with play. The puppy is supposed to concentrate and understand what it went out for. It is there to pee, not to fool around and incidentally relieve itself. Don't do anything to take its mind off the task at hand. Your chore is quite simple:
1. Take the puppy out.
2. Watch to make sure it relieves itself.
3. Praise it.
4. Take it back inside.

Believe me, the time you spend outdoors in the dark or in the rain is a very important learning experience for your dog. And with time everything gets easier. Even tiny puppies don't dirty the place where they sleep. As soon as they can walk they toddle into a corner of the box to pee there, far away from their bed or play area. As your puppy gradually learns that your house is the place where one sleeps and eats, it also learns not to use it as a bathroom.

Be consistent. Stop your puppy every time it tries to go to the bathroom in the wrong place. Be sure always to praise it if it does what it is supposed to do. Always use the same words and commands. Every time someone is too lazy to be consistent, this signals to the puppy that maybe this whole business isn't so important after all. If you are not predictable and reliable, how can you expect your dog to be so?

When your puppy is about sixteen weeks old, it begins to gain control over its bladder. If you have a regular routine of taking it out, the puppy will probably start using its box less all on

its own because it relieves itself enough outdoors. As soon as you notice that the box hardly gets any use any longer, take it away. It has served its purpose. Your dog now understands what you have been trying to teach it. Congratulations!

Walking on the Leash

Most puppies don't particularly enjoy their first outing on the leash. They keep sitting down, try to scratch the stupid collar off, and lunge in every direction, almost strangling themselves in the process. Or they may become completely hysterical, throw their entire weight against collar and leash, and finally lie flat on their stomachs because they simply can't stand the leash anymore. A puppy gets used to collar and leash most easily if it can wear them for some time without anyone at the other end of the leash. Let it wander around the

Walking on the leash takes practice...

...sometimes you take off in the wrong direction

apartment wearing the collar, and then attach a very light leash (such as a leash meant for cats), so it can get used to the feeling. Pick up the leash now and then and walk around behind the dog without its feeling any tension on the collar. Squat down on the floor and pull gently on the leash and at the same time call the puppy to you. This way it will very soon realize that this extension of your arm that reaches all the way to its collar is nothing to be afraid of.

The squatting position is not particularly comfortable for humans, but it is unavoidable if you want to teach your little dog any commands. It is not easy for a puppy to understand what it is you want it to do if all it can see of you is from the knees down. After all, it doesn't speak your language and has to rely on your facial expression for cues. So it has to be able to recognize your expression somehow.

When you take your dog

...and wonder why your way isn't just as good...

...and almost strangle yourself.

outside, avoid pulling it by the leash. Being yanked by the leash makes most dogs panic. Encourage your puppy instead with enthusiastic praise and jumping up and down. Laud it extravagantly if it does follow you, and try to make as little use of the leash as possible. During

Come!

Come! is really the easiest of the commands if you start teaching it early enough. Puppies are easily convinced that you are the most interesting object in their vicinity. Let your puppy follow you around, first

companion, a fact that works in your favor.) Change directions and bend down now and then to pet your puppy. Don't stop once the puppy has caught on and follows you well. You want to establish a firm habit, so keep going. When it's meal time and the puppy is in another room, perhaps helping the children with their homework, call its name and rattle its food dish. You'll be amazed how quickly your puppy will appear. Dogs learn to recognize the sounds associated with food incredibly fast.

If your puppy is preoccupied with something else or playing with a toy, squat down near it, open your arms wide, and call it in a friendly tone. It will immediately drop everything and come running up to you (wouldn't you do the same?). Then praise it and cuddle it and let it go again. That was all you wanted of it. Surprise it several times a day with such bursts of affection—but the puppy has to come **to you** when you call.

Draw the puppy's attention to you either by making some kind of noise

At the beginning you have to crouch down to talk to your puppy.

these first lessons it doesn't matter at all which side of you the puppy is on, whether it is walking in a straight line, and if it sits down on your left when you stop.

indoors, then, if possible, outside. Walk slowly, click your tongue, and call your puppy's name in a bright, cheerful voice, adding the word *come!* Practice walking around like this every day with the dog following. (Puppies are anxious not to lose their primary human

yourself or by arousing its interest with a squeaky toy, then walk or run away, turning around to call the dog. When it comes, bend down to praise and pet it exuberantly and at length. With a very young puppy you have to run in slow motion; with larger dogs you may want to practice outdoors. Wherever or however you do it, you will get your dog's attention.

Running Away

This is a favorite game of cocky young dogs. It's called "Let's see how fast Master or Mistress can run!" and is associated in the dog's mind with "Come when you're called." Some puppies, especially when they notice that their owner is in a hurry or getting nervous, turn on their heel and take off as fast as they can in the opposite direction or in big circles around you. You will never win in this game, though you will get plenty of exercise. Every time you reach out to grab hold of your cute little puppy, it will dash off at the last moment to keep the game going a while longer.

The secret is never to get this game started in the first place. Instead, make sure your puppy sees you turning away, apparently acting on higher intelligence, and walking off quickly in the opposite direction while issuing a sharp *come!* over your shoulder. The puppy is confused now. You are obviously not playing the game according to the rules and, worse, you seem to want to leave your tiny little dog behind in the wilds where anything might happen to it. In no time at all your puppy will put two and two together and come running after you. When it reaches you and as you put it on the leash, praise it extravagantly, no matter how seriously you may have contemplated wringing its little neck a moment ago. Don't forget: **The first time you scold or discipline your puppy when it comes to you is the last time it comes to you in cheerful anticipation.**

Thinking Like a Dog

In order to do justice to your dog and to be able to train it, reward it, and discipline it in a way that makes sense to

Walk slowly and call your puppy in a cheerful tone.

Fox Terrier

dog will know that *come!* doesn't mean the fun is over now. Your dog should have the sense that coming when called is always worthwhile. Always call it with a purpose, and heap praise on it every time it obeys.

Rewards and Punishment

All of obedience training is based on positive and negative reinforcement. Rewards that evoke a rush of good feeling help make the execution of commands attractive, and the point of negative reinforcement is to convince your dog not to repeat undesirable behavior.

The trick is to figure out how to use rewards and punishment most effectively. If you want to find out how to go about praising and disciplining a puppy, watch a mother dog. Her punishments and rewards are swift, immediate, and always just; and the puppies understand precisely which behavior they are expected to repeat and which not. And they get the point instantly. Puppies hardly ever

the canine mind, you have to try to think like a dog. Of course, to expect the dog to reciprocate is sheer anthropomorphizing and pointless. But if you think like a dog and make its logic your own, you will hardly ever go wrong in your training efforts. In practice this means: Don't call your dog if you are going to stick it in the bathtub, clean its ears, take its temperature, or give it horrible-tasting medicine. Never call it to punish it. Don't call it after you have just let it off the leash a minute ago to play with other dogs. Don't keep calling it over and over again

to see if it obeys. Train your dog, but don't overdo it. Think logically. Think like a dog. If something unpleasant happens to the dog after it has come to you, it will think twice in the future before coming and come only reluctantly when you call.

Call it instead when it's time to eat, to pet it, to play with it, to take it for a walk. After you have let it off the leash to play with other dogs, wait ten minutes before you call it back; praise it when it comes, and **immediately** let it go back to play again. If you do this two or three times every time you take it walking in the park, your

misunderstand their mother, and they never deliberately ignore her or pretend not to hear. That's how good a mother dog is at conveying her message.

You don't have to act exactly like a mother dog. You probably have little desire to grab the puppy by the scruff of its neck with your teeth to give it a good shake. But you can imitate the canine approach to education to help you establish communication with your puppy. Without communication there can be no teaching. Praise is a way of communicating, and you can never praise a puppy too much. Always make a great fuss whenever it does anything you consider desirable. Tell it how proud you are of it, how it is the cleverest puppy that ever lived. Later, when your dog has grown up or has the commands down pat, you don't have to congratulate it every time it sits, comes, and so on. At some point all this becomes normal, and the dog does what is expected of it without further ado. But as long as the dog still has to get used to commands and as long as obeying is still not completely automatic, no amount of encouragement is too much.

It is also possible to motivate dogs with edible rewards. You call the dog, it comes, and it gets a biscuit. The dog sits, and it gets a biscuit. You can use edible rewards to reinforce a command now and then. But one often doesn't have the biscuits handy when one needs them, and besides your dog will get in the habit of begging and staring at your coat pocket. More importantly though, your dog should concentrate on your voice and body language, not your coat or pants pocket. Voice and physical affection are a wonderful way to convey approval if they are used correctly. What words you use are of no importance whatsoever. Whether you praise your dog in English, Lithuanian, or Portuguese makes no difference at all. It's the tone that counts. Talking to your dog in a lively, upbeat voice has an animating and encouraging effect on it, whereas a somber, threatening tone will feel like a rebuke. Be aware of how loudly you speak to your dog. If you shout at it all the time or

Mother's punishments are swift, just, and never half-hearted.

yell after it, it will think this is your normal voice and soon fail to be impressed by it. (You can observe the same phenomenon of simply not reacting anymore in children who are always being called by their mother. I call this "mother deafness.") In most cases a "No!" thundered with such emphasis that the dog thinks the earth is about to split open under its paws will do. Sometimes you may have to resort to physical discipline if your dog has done something truly appalling—stealing from the table, going through the garbage, chewing on your evening dress, or swallowing your pet hamster.

Physical punishment is a difficult subject. No one likes to punish or beat his or her dog. We have all heard horrendous stories about sadistic dog owners, about unscrupulous dog trainers, and about dogs so traumatized that they end up biting out of fear. As a result most people discipline their dogs only halfheartedly because they don't know how to do it properly, with the consequence that their dogs do more or less as they please. I myself was once told my name would be turned in to the ASPCA when I smacked my Weimaraner female on the behind because she was chasing a bicyclist. This is a dog as unlikely to bite out of fear as can be imagined and one of the most self-confident animals I know.

Sometimes **physical punishment** is called for, but only in the following situations:

◆ if your dog is growling at someone, attacking, chasing, or snapping,

Edible treats are very effective, but it's better to use them sparingly.

◆ if it steals food off the table,
◆ if it keeps destroying things,
◆ if it bites other dogs.

If you do have to resort to physical punishment, you have to do it right. The actual force exerted is less important than the proper timing, a certain amount of drama, and taking the dog by surprise.

Many people use objects to smack a dog with, most commonly the proverbial rolled-up newspaper. I myself consider this a mistake. A mother dog doesn't go looking for a newspaper when she wants to discipline a puppy. When she notices a puppy wobbling beyond the radius she considers safe, she puts a front paw on its neck and pushes the puppy down. In more serious cases, she briefly uses her teeth, with more or less force. You should follow the same principle. The hand that feeds and pets is also the hand that punishes. Dogs that are disciplined in accordance with canine logic—in a way, that is, that the puppy can understand—are never afraid of the

human hand. Only dogs that experience their master or mistress as an unpredictable and unreasonable being or who are not punished until hours after some wrong-doing develop that fear. Never spank your dog from behind; it is very important to have eye contact with your dog when you scold or discipline it.

Punishment must **always** follow on the heels of the crime; it must be administered when you catch your dog in the act of misbehaving and only then. Dogs have a very short memory. If you realize that your dog ate the cheesecake an hour ago, it's too late for punishment. Your dog would have no idea what you are talking about even if you wave the empty pie plate in front of its face a hundred times. Don't imagine that your dog has a bad conscience if you show it the sofa cushion it has torn to shreds. If the dog flattens its ears, looks sideways, or cowers, it is only responding to your angry body posture, and with good reason! But this will not stop it from disemboweling another sofa cushion the next time it feels

bored. It had no clue what was the matter when you yelled "No!" and showed it the remains of the cushion. Were you upset because you didn't like the feathers? Did you want the cushion to be in a different place? Or what? Dogs have no such thing as a bad conscience because they don't have the same moral sense of good and bad that we have. Next time your dog has to stay home alone, leave it in a place where it can't get at things it is not supposed to eat. Put it in the playpen, in the kitchen, or the hall.

Next time you catch your dog about to rip up a cushion, grab it gently by the scruff of the neck, lift it up a little, and carefully shake it back and forth quickly and firmly a few times while you slowly lower it to the ground again. Look your dog straight in the eyes while you do this, and shout "No!" in a thunderous voice. ***Note: Always use <u>extreme caution</u> when disciplining very young puppies.*** Mother dogs shake their pups by the scruff of their necks when they want to discipline them and show them in

American Staffordshire Terriers

unmistakable terms who is boss. The shaking may mean that it's time to stop wrestling, that the teats are off limits now, or that Mother is to be left in peace. Being shaken like this is an uncomfortable and undignified experience for a puppy. There you hang like an idiot, unable even to struggle. After undergoing the treatment, puppies normally lie on their backs with their legs sticking up in the air. Few of them will repeat whatever it was that evoked this punishment.

Shaking is, however, a punishment reserved only for *very serious* offenses and extreme situations. It serves to emphasize your position as the alpha member in the pack. For less serious offenses, **verbal scolding** will suffice, which means an emphatic "No!" Your voice should sound very sharp, loud, and commanding. Some dog owners have a natural verbal dominance, but anyone can learn to sound reasonably authoritative. Pronounce your "No!" as though you were hurling a

verbal rock at your dog. No complaining, no begging. You don't argue with dogs and you don't nag them. These approaches have not the slightest effect on them.

Making Peace Again

After you have chastised your dog, you have to make peace again. For at least fifteen minutes—or, with dogs six months or older, half an hour—after you have disciplined your dog, you should remain completely

passive, refraining from speaking to it, petting it, and having eye contact. Your dog will probably be looking away from you, studying the floor, or looking as though it is trying to crawl into a crack between the floor boards. These are normal expressions of submission and should not be cut short or interrupted. Most dog owners make the mistake of trying to console their dog as soon as it acts this way by going up to it and petting it. If the dog remains immobile or begins to tremble, the owner suffers even greater pangs of conscience. What is actually happening is that your dog needs a little time to digest what just happened. Leave it alone now. After a while it will come up to you on its own initiative. (If your dog comes trotting up to you to be petted five minutes after having been disciplined, then you should reconsider whether the punishment was forceful enough, because the dog was apparently not particularly impressed by it.)

But no matter how wretchedly a puppy behaved, its mother always forgives it. She never refuses to feed it.

It is not sent to bed without supper. Nor does she slip it a little treat or some extra dessert under the table as a reward for good behavior. Eating is one thing; teaching, another. Mother knows that best.

Sit!

Sit! and *down!* are the two most important commands your puppy has to learn. They make your life together immeasurably easier and serve as a basis for more advanced commands. If your dog is sitting, it can't jump up on visitors, chase after strange cats, race out the door, or run into the road.

Put your puppy on the leash so that it will stay very close to you. Then command *sit!* and simultaneously press down on its rump. As soon as it is sitting, praise it. Repeat the exercise over and over in the course of the day: when putting on the leash—*sit!*; when crossing the street (before stepping off the curb)—*sit!*; before putting down the food dish—*sit!* (You are also the one who decides when it can get up

again, namely, only after the explicit command *come!*); before giving a biscuit—*sit!*; when playing together, make the dog *sit!* every so often. You will be surprised how quickly your puppy will master this command, especially in connection with the food bowl.

Down!

This command is best taught in combination with *sit!* When your puppy is sitting, pull the leash forward and downward until the puppy is forced to lie down. As soon as it begins to lie down, say *"Down!"* Praise the puppy, and have it lie there until you release it with the command *come!* If your dog keeps trying to get up, put your foot on the leash to keep it from rising, and praise it. This command, too, has to be practiced a number of times during the day, but without making a big deal of it.

Stay!

Stay! is a command that is absolutely crucial for your dog to obey, especially when it is not on the leash. If this command is mastered, you can let your dog off the leash and move away without it following you. This is especially useful when you have to run after your children, when you have obstinate cows to deal with, when you want to get the horses in from the pasture, when you look to see if any cars are coming at an intersection, and so on. But you have to wait until your dog is at least six months old to practice *stay!* And with slow learners or particularly pesky adolescents you may have to wait until they have become a little more responsive and trustworthy.

Start practicing this command first in a quiet place, such as your living room or the hall. Put the dog on the leash and have it lie down. Then command *stay!* and walk quietly around the dog. As soon as it makes a motion to rise, say

Sit! is usually learned quickly.

To teach Down! keep the dog on the leash and have it Sit!...

"*Stay!*" again. Then jump up and down in front of it but don't allow it to get up; walk around it in a bigger circle and, finally, release it with a *come!* and lots of praise. As soon as the dog has mastered this lesson, put the leash down next to the dog after telling it to lie down and stay, and walk away a few steps.

Heel!

You can start practicing *heel!* from the very beginning. As soon as the puppy knows how to walk on the leash, let it walk only on your left side. (This is a relic from past times when a woman walked on a man's right side and the saber and the dog were on his left. Nowadays women walk wherever they want, sabers have become quite rare, and only dogs still walk on the left side; this is so the world over, even though nobody knows the reason why any longer.) When you say "*Heel!*" keep the dog on a very short line, so that it has to walk with its shoulder next to your knee (or ankle, depending on the size of

...then pull the puppy forward by the leash so that it has to lie down; as soon as it starts to lie down...

...say "Down!"

your dog). Let the dog get ahead of you again a few inches, then tighten the leash for a second, repeat *heel!*, then release the pressure when the dog has regained its proper position. If it then proceeds to walk a few steps without pulling, praise it and give some slack to the line. Repeat the exercise a little later. As soon as your dog has learned to heel on the leash, you can start practicing the command without the leash.

But keep the leash in your left hand, and perhaps have a few dog biscuits handy, so that your dog gets the idea that running alongside you is much more exciting than paying attention to those kids playing over there. Keep asking your dog to heel as you walk in circles and figure eights and around trees—your puppy always at your knee or ankle. Be lavish with praise, give the dog its biscuit, and go through the exercise again half an hour later.

The same rule applies as in all the other lessons: the more often you go over an exercise, the sooner your puppy will think of the command and its execution as something perfectly normal and ordinary. Don't institute specific lesson times; instead incorporate the training into your normal activities throughout the day. But don't overdo it. Your puppy is still a baby, with limited powers of concentration. And most important of all, don't get irritated if your puppy doesn't understand something, refuses to concentrate, or tries to

Basset Hound

distract you. It is still very young. Take a deep breath, finish the exercise, and quit. Tomorrow is another day. Perhaps a better day.

Perfection

In conclusion let me say: **Every dog owner has the dog he or she deserves.** It doesn't matter how well behaved your dog is, as long as it is exactly the way you want it to be. It doesn't matter if your dog sleeps in

To heel! the dog has to walk along next to your left knee (or ankle).

your bed and gets buttered toast for breakfast, as long as it behaves in a civilized manner and as long as this is what you want. I myself have three goals in training my dogs. Their behavior has to be

1. good enough so that life with them is comfortable and peaceful,
2. good enough so other people are not bothered, and
3. good enough so that they cause no harm to themselves or to people or other dogs.

As long as my dogs adhere to these limits, I'm perfectly content. My dogs have to be well enough trained to fit harmoniously into my life, in which frequent traveling, other animals and people, parties, and visiting play a large part. Some of my dogs insist on learning tricks and other skills my other dogs would never dream of. Some of them had to be trained very strictly, with much vocal thunder and alpha behavior on my part, while others practically trained themselves. But they all have mastered—and act according to—the basic social manners necessary for living together.

Neapolitan Mastiff

Every dog owner has to find out for him- or herself how much sternness or gentleness is required for training any particular dog. And how meticulously a dog should be trained is also up to each individual dog owner. As in every other arena of life, things start to get really interesting once you get beyond the basics. Many people find great satisfaction in teaching their dogs all kinds of skills. It is thrilling to watch eager dogs hurl themselves with utter concentration through an agility course, accompanied by their breathless owners. Anywhere where dogs and their owners congregate you can tell those that form a real team at a glance. Dog sledding has developed into a serious sport. The possibilities are almost endless. It is just a question of what you want—and where your dog's talents lie. The more you learn about your puppy and its breed, the more you will realize that the only limits there are have to do with you: how much time and money you want to invest to have as much fun as possible with your four-legged and probably still rather wobbly new family member. The training suggestions I have given you cover only the most basic and important skills a puppy has to master in order to behave in a civilized manner in the world of humans. What your puppy will ultimately turn into is up to you.

Rules for Disciplining

◆ Puppies are intelligent, quick thinking animals, but they may not understand what you are asking. Remember the age and experience of your student!

◆ Discipline your puppy with voice modulation and tone. Don't resort to shouting and never hit the dog.

◆ Always start with a simple, single-word command for a simple exercise.

◆ Don't nag, argue, or try to reason with any dog.

◆ If the pup doesn't understand, change tasks.

◆ Ignoring the pup is the strongest discipline you'll ever need!

Appendix

Useful Addresses and Literature

Associations

American Humane Organization
9725 East Hampton Avenue
Denver, CO 80231

American Kennel Club (AKC)
260 Madison Avenue
New York, NY 10016
www.akc.org
[For registration, records, or litter information, write:
5580 Centerview Drive
Raleigh, NC 27606]

American Veterinary Medical Association
930 North Meacham Road
Schaumburg, IL 60173

Canadian Kennel Club
111 Eglington Avenue
Toronto 12, Ontario
CANADA

National Dog Registry (tattoo, microchip)
P.O. Box 116
Woodstock, NY 12498

Periodicals

AKC Gazette
51 Madison Avenue
New York, NY 10010

Dog Fancy Magazine
P.O. Box 53264
Boulder, CO 80322-3264

Dog World
29 North Wacker Drive
Chicago, IL 60606

Books

American Kennel Club. *The Complete Dog Book*. New York: Macmillan Publishing Co., 1992.

Coile, Caroline D. *Encyclopedia of Dog Breeds*. Hauppauge, New York: Barron's Educational Series, Inc., 1998.

Rice, Dan. *The Dog Handbook*. Hauppauge, New York: Barron's Educational Series, Inc., 1999.

von der Leyen, Katharina. *Illustrated Guide to 140 Dog Breeds*. Hauppauge, New York: Barron's Educational Series, Inc., 2000.

Yarden, Miriam. *Hey Pup, Let's Talk!* Hauppauge, New York: Barron's Educational Series, Inc., 2000.

Appendix

Index

Appendix

Appendix

Appendix

Appendix

Everyone gets the dog he or she deserves.

Appendix

Original title of the book in German is
Das Welpenbuch.
Translated from the German by Rita and Robert
Kimber.

All inquiries should be addressed to:
Barron's Educational Series, Inc.
250 Wireless Boulevard
Hauppauge, NY 11788
http://www.barronseduc.com

International Standard Book No. 0-7641-1601-0

Library of Congress Catalog Card No. 00-064195

Library of Congress Cataloging-in-Publication Data
Von der Leyen, Katharina.
   [Welpenbuch. English]
   Puppies / Katharina von der Leyen.
        p. cm.
   Includes bibliographical references (p.).
   ISBN 0-7641-1601-0
   1. Puppies. I. Title.

SF427.V5913 2001
636.7'07—dc21   00-064195

Printed in Hong Kong
9 8 7 6 5 4 3

Photo Credits

Archiv Boiselle / Bacchella: all photos, except
Animal Photography / Thompson: 25l, 25r
Animal Photography / Willbie: 24r, 27r
G. Boiselle: 28–37 (all)
T. Morgan: 146r, 147l, 147r
H. Reinhard: 22l
Ch. Steiner: 22r, 53, 55, 57o, 57u, 58, 59, 68, 74, 76,
    78, 84, 90, 120u, 123, 130, 132, 136/137, 138, 139,
    140, 142, 146l, 149

Cover Photos:
Animals Animals: front cover, inside front cover, inside
    back cover.
Archiv Boiselle/Bacchella: back cover

Photo p. 1:   Golden Retriever
Photo p. 2/3:   Great Pyrenees
Photo p. 8:   Great Dane
Photo p. 28:   Crossbreeds
                (Great Dane/Irish Wolfhound)
Photo p. 38:   Cocker Spaniel
Photo p. 50:   Italian Mountain Hound
Photo p. 64:   West Highland White Terrier
Photo p. 80:   Siberian Husky
Photo p. 92:   Dalmatian
Photo p. 102:   Labrador Retriever
Photo p. 126:   German Wire-Hair
Photo p. 152:   Griffon